# SEXUALLY TRANSMITTED DISEASES

## by Salvatore Tocci

Franklin Watts
A DIVISION OF GROLIER PUBLISHING
New York · London · Hong Kong · Sydney
Danbury, Connecticut

Photographs©: AP/Wide World Photos: 40 (Doug Mills), 93 (Doug Pizac), 65 (Pat Sullivan); Corbis-Bettmann: 91; Liaison Agency, Inc.: 96 (Stephen Ferry), 98 (Ed Lallo); Peter Arnold Inc.: 25 (SIU); Photo Researchers: 41 (Chris Bjornberg), 20 (Peter Gull), 19 (Carlyn Iverson), cover, 1 (Dr. Kari Lounatmaa/SPL), 129 (Will & Deni McIntyre), 119 (James Prince), 127 (SIU), 53, 56 (St. Bartholomew's Hospital/SPL), 14 (St. Mary's Hospital Medical School/SPL), 94 (St. Stephen's Hospital, London/SPL); Stock Boston: 48, 62, 111, 124 (Bob Daemmrich), 45 (Lawrence Migdale); The Stock Market: 87 (C.B.P.), 109 (John Henley), 8 (Tom & Dee Ann McCarthy); Visuals Unlimited: 10 (Kathy Talaro), 74.

Visit Franklin Watts on the Internet at:
http://publishing.grolier.com

Interior design by Kathleen Santini

Library of Congress Cataloging-in-Publication Data

Tocci, Salvatore
    Sexually transmitted diseases / Salvatore Tocci.
      p. cm.
    Includes bibliographical references and index.
     ISBN 0-531-11590-9
   1. Sexually transmitted diseases--Juvenile literature.
[1. Sexually transmitted diseases.] I Title.

RC200.25 .T63 2001
616.95'1--dc21

                        00-039927

# Table of Contents

# Introduction

Most Americans are not aware that an epidemic is spreading rapidly throughout the country. Anyone—a factory employee, a farmworker, or an average teenager—can become infected. In fact, teenagers are often the main targets of this epidemic. Many of those who become infected are innocent victims. Often they do not even know they have become infected because nothing unusual happens to them. The epidemic, however, has not gone unnoticed by everyone. Many health officials have become aware of the epidemic and are concerned, but no plans have been made to stop or even control it. What these health officials are concerned about is an epidemic of **sexually transmitted diseases**, known simply as **STDs**.

A sexually transmitted disease, or STD, is usually a result of some form of sexual activity. No doubt you have heard of one such STD—**AIDS**. For almost 20 years, AIDS has been known as the deadliest STD that people have ever faced, not only in America but all over the world. Billions of dollars have been spent in an effort to stop the spread of AIDS and cure those who have become infected. Scientists throughout the world have tirelessly pursued ways to make people immune to the disease. The media has reported numerous stories about people with AIDS, in the hope of making others more aware of this deadly disease. Although people are now very much  aware of AIDS, there is still no way to make a person immune to the disease—and no way to cure a person who has become infected with it. But AIDS is not the whole story.

Health officials are also concerned about other STDs that are rapidly spreading, just like AIDS. Unlike AIDS, however, these STDs are not receiving much attention and therefore are causing a "silent" epidemic. What really concerns health officials is that some of these STDs, like AIDS, can be deadly if left untreated. Moreover, these STDS are known to contribute to a form of cancer in women, known as cervical cancer. These STDs also contribute to infant death and adult infertility. Infertility means that an adult is physically unable to have children of his or her own. Finally, people infected with certain STDs are two to five times more likely than others to develop AIDS. People who have both AIDS and another STD are more infectious and thus more likely to spread these diseases.

While the spread of each STD follows its own pattern, the overall picture is grim. The incidence of some STDs in the United States far exceeds that in any other developed country. The rates are especially high in rural and inner-city areas where access to proper medical care is limited. A recent study revealed that chlamydia is spreading most rapidly, especially among teenagers. In 1998, researchers at Johns Hopkins University in Baltimore, Maryland, reported that nearly 30 percent of females ages 12 to 19 tested positive for chlamydia. The Centers for Disease Control and Prevention (CDC) estimates that in 1999 four million Americans became infected with chlamydia. From 1987 to 1996, the rate of infections for this STD increased more than 400 percent. Although not as drastic, the rates for other STDs are also increasing rapidly. Just why are these STDs spreading so rapidly?

For one thing, many people are reluctant to talk about them. The reason is that these diseases are spread primarily through sexual contact and mainly affect the sex organs of the body. As a result, an infected person is often embarrassed to admit having an STD and may be unwilling to seek medical treatment. Also, most STDs do not produce any signs or symptoms so the person does not know they are infected. Thus, a person may unknowingly spread the STD to someone else. In turn, this person may pass the disease on to yet another person. As a result, the STD continues to spread. The general public, however, is not totally responsible for the spread of STDs. A recent study revealed that 60 percent of the doctors surveyed do not routinely check their new patients for an STD. These doctors feel that STDs do not usually occur in the kind of person they see as patients. Without being given the proper medical tests, a number of their patients are likely to contribute to the spread of STDs.

To control and eventually stop the spread of STDs, two things are required—knowledge and motivation. A person must know about the different types of STDs, how they are caused, exactly how they can be transmitted, what symptoms to look for, and what treatments are available. As you have just read, anyone can get an STD, so everyone must have this information. Perhaps those who need this knowledge most are teenagers. Today, more and more teenagers are having sex at an earlier age than ever before. This means that many more teenagers are exposed to STDs than ever before. Teenagers are also less likely to tell anyone that

*Many teenagers today are likely to experience sex–and possibly, an STD–soon after puberty.*

they have become infected with an STD, mainly because they do not realize it.

In addition to knowledge, people must have the motivation to change any behavior that promotes the spread of STDs. Here's where this book can be most useful. We will discuss the main details about the major STDs responsible for today's epidemic. You will learn about their causes, symptoms, effects, and treatments. Knowing what these diseases can do might give you the motivation to change any behavior that can spread an STD. With such knowledge and motivation, you may be able to contribute to controlling, and perhaps even eliminating, this "silent" epidemic.

# The Invaders

To understand what causes STDs, you must first look into the world of microscopic creatures known as **microorganisms**. As its name implies, a microorganism is a living thing so tiny that you need a microscope to see it. Included among the microorganisms are bacteria. A **bacterium** (**bacteria**, plural) is a small, single cell, the simplest form of life. A typical bacterium measures only 1 micrometer (0.0000003 inch) in diameter. To get some idea of how small this is, it would take more than 250 bacteria to form a speck large enough to see with your eyes. But despite their small size, some bacteria are capable of causing serious diseases, including various STDs, in humans. If left untreated, some of these diseases might result in death.

Today we have no trouble believing that such tiny organisms can cause disease and death. We even have a special name for these microorganisms—germs. But just over 100 years ago, most people laughed at the suggestion that organisms so small could cause disease in humans. At that time very few people, including doctors, believed in the germ theory, even though the existence of microorganisms had been known since the 1600s.

Microorganisms were first observed in 1676 by a Dutch lens maker named Anton van Leeuwenhoek. Using a tiny lens as a magnifying glass, Leeuwenhoek examined a wide variety of specimens, including drops of pond water. He reported seeing

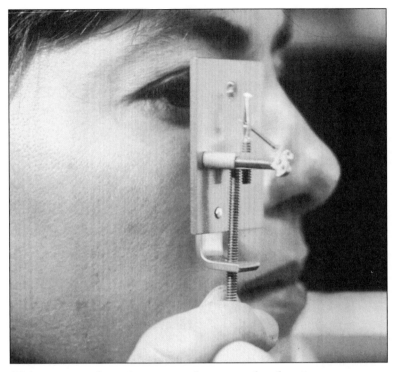

*This woman is using a van Leeuwenhoek microscope.*

tiny creatures swimming around in the pond water. His observations were impressive, especially when you consider the crude microscope Leeuwenhoek was using.

Nearly 200 years passed after Leeuwenhoek's work before a connection was made between microorganisms and disease. That link was forged in the 1800s by scientists working throughout Europe. Louis Pasteur, a French chemist, identified the microorganisms that caused various diseases in both animals and humans. In England, Joseph Lister showed the importance of cleaning surgical wounds with a special solution that killed germs. In Germany, Robert Koch proved that specific microorganisms caused certain infections and diseases. In Austria, Ignaz Semmelweis demonstrated the need for doctors to wash their hands and instruments thoroughly before delivering a baby. Taken together, the work of Pasteur, Lister, Koch, and Semmelweis left no doubt—germs cause disease and death.

Not all microorganisms, however, cause disease or death. In fact, many are beneficial. Some bacteria acts as nature's recyclers by decomposing dead plants and animals and returning the raw materials to the ground. Some bacteria enable plants to obtain the materials they need to carry out photosynthesis. Some bacteria are used in the processing of various foods like yogurt, cheese, and olives. And some bacteria  live in our intestines and make vitamins that we need. But unfortunately, bacteria do not always interact with humans in a helpful way.

Bacteria that are harmful are known as **pathogens**. A pathogen is a microorganism that can cause an infection or disease in humans. Pathogens exist everywhere in the world. They thrive on land, living on objects you touch and in foods you eat. They live in water—rivers, streams, oceans, and even in the water you drink. They float in the air you breathe. You cannot avoid bacterial pathogens. Every day, these bacterial pathogens invade your body.

## Bacteria

Bacteria are among the most successful organisms on Earth. They can live everywhere in the world, from the frozen regions of Antarctica to the scorching deserts of Africa. Bacteria have been discovered miles below Earth's surface and in deep ocean waters. And no matter where they are, bacteria thrive. They divide rapidly to produce new bacteria. Some bacteria divide as many as five times in one hour. If you were to place one bacteria in a laboratory dish that contained an abundant supply of food, you would find more than 600,000 bacteria in the dish after only four hours. After six hours, you would find about 475 million bacteria in the dish!

There are nearly 5,000 different kinds of bacteria, but they come in basically three shapes. Some bacteria are round or oval. These bacteria are called *cocci*. You are probably familiar with one kind of cocci bacteria—*streptococci* —which cause a severe throat infection known as "strep throat." *Pneumococci* bacteria cause the serious lung infection known as pneumonia. Other types of bacteria are shaped like rods. The bacteria in your intestine that produce vitamins are shaped like rods. Still other types of bacteria have a spiral shape like a corkscrew. These spiral-shaped bacteria are very difficult to see under an ordinary microscope.

Before bacteria are examined with a microscope, they are stained or dyed to make them more visible. The steps involved in staining bacteria were developed by a Danish scientist named Hans Gram. In the first step, the wall that surrounds a bacterial cell is stained with a purple dye. The last step involves rinsing the bacterial cells with alcohol. Some bacteria have a thick cell wall that retains the purple dye even after being rinsed with alcohol. These cells are referred to as gram-positive. Some bacteria have a thin wall that does not hold on to the purple stain when the cells are rinsed with alcohol. These cells are colored pink from a dye that is applied after the alcohol rinse. Cells that have the pink stain are referred to as gram-negative. Both round and rod-shaped bacteria are either gram-positive or gram-negative. In either case, the stain makes the bacteria easier to see under a microscope. But spiral-shaped bacteria do not absorb either the purple or pink stain. Scientists must use a special microscope to see these bacteria.

All bacteria must get into the body before they can cause disease. Some enter through a cut in the skin. Others make their way into the body through the nose when they are inhaled in tiny droplets of water. Some bacteria are present in the foods we eat or the water we drink. Exchange of bodily fluids such as blood can also introduce bacteria into the body. Bacteria that cause STDs enter the body as a result of sexual contact.

Once inside the body, bacterial pathogens begin to destroy cells and tiny blood vessels in the area they enter. Some bacteria release chemical poisons called **toxins**. Toxins interfere with various processes that normally take place in the body. For example, one toxin produced by bacteria interferes with the ability of nerve cells to carry messages.

To fight a bacterial invasion, your body's immune system is called into action. The workings of the immune system are complex, but basically the immune system sends in armies of white blood cells to destroy the bacterial invaders. There are different types of white blood cells. Some white blood cells destroy bacteria directly. Other types of white blood cells release chemicals that clump or round up the bacteria, making it easier for them to be destroyed. The area of the body where all of this takes place becomes sore and swollen. All this activity also causes the body temperature to rise. So a fever is an indication that there is an infection somewhere in the body.

If the immune system is successful, the bacterial invaders are destroyed and the infection is over. The body then begins to replace the cells and blood vessels that were destroyed. This is what happens when an infected cut heals, or a sore throat gets better. In some cases, however, the immune system cannot overcome the bacterial invaders. The bacteria enter the bloodstream where they cause **septicemia**, or blood poisoning. Traveling in the blood, the bacteria can spread throughout the body. They can then infect other organs such as the brain, kidneys, liver, or lungs. Once inside an organ, the bacteria thrive and multiply.

In the past, there was nothing that could be done for a bacterial infection. Even though doctors recognized that microorganisms could cause disease and death, they had no methods to fight an infection that had spread. Millions of people died when these microscopic invaders escaped the body's immune system. But in 1928 a Scottish scientist named Alexander Fleming made a very

*Sir Alexander Fleming working in his laboratory*

important observation that would change this story. Fleming noticed that bacteria were not growing near a mold that had formed in some culture dishes. Fleming reasoned that the mold was releasing a chemical substance that killed the bacteria in its vicinity. He isolated the substance and named it *penicillin*. During World War II, penicillin saved millions of soldiers' lives. Since that time, penicillin has saved countless more.

Penicillin is an **antibiotic**. An antibiotic is a chemical substance that is used as a drug to kill pathogenic bacteria. In effect, antibiotics "turn the tables" on bacteria. Just as bacterial pathogens interfere with processes that normally occur in the body, antibiotics interfere with processes that are normally carried out by bacteria. For example, penicillin works by preventing bacteria from forming the wall that surrounds the bacterial cell. Without this wall, the cell is more vulnerable to attack. Since the discovery of penicillin, other antibiotics have been discovered or produced chemically. The choice of which antibiotic to use depends in part on whether the bacteria is gram-positive or gram-negative.

Antibiotics have formed an effective weapon that has helped control various diseases caused by bacterial pathogens. These diseases include tuberculosis, bacterial pneumonia, and several STDs that we will discuss later. Unfortunately, the story of antibiotics does not end here. In recent years, an increasing number of bacteria have become resistant to the antibiotics that once killed them. This resistance has developed as a natural response to the widespread use of antibiotics for so many years. Upon exposure to an antibiotic, most bacteria are killed, but some bacteria are resistant to the antibiotic. These bacteria survive and produce more bacteria, which are also resistant. Over time, more and more antibiotic-resistant bacteria are produced. Use of the same antibiotic is no longer as effective. Scientists are currently looking for new antibiotics to combat bacterial invaders that have become resistant. Keep in mind that antibiotics are effective only against bacteria. Antibiotics are useless against other types of invaders.

## Other Single-Celled Invaders

Bacteria are not the only microscopic invaders that can cause disease and death. Another organism that can affect a human's health is a **protist**. A protist is a single-celled organism that is more complex than a bacterium. Protists are responsible for malaria, a disease that affects 100 million people in the world and kills 1 million people, mostly children, every year. A number of other diseases are also caused by protists, including sleeping sickness and Chagas' disease, which involves severe heart damage. A protist known as trichomonas is responsible for one type of STD. This protist infects both males and females. Trichomonas can be passed back and forth between two people who have frequent sexual contact, making treatment difficult.

Another single-celled organism that can affect human health is **yeast**. Yeasts are single-celled organisms that grow in colonies. One type of yeast is commonly found in various areas of the body, including the mouth and intestines. Inside the body, this yeast normally exists in balance with other microorganisms, such as bacteria. However, under certain conditions, this yeast can cause an infection, especially in women. Because an antibiotic

16

would be useless in treating a yeast infection, a doctor prescribes a medication that is specifically effective against yeast.

## Viruses

Another type of invader is something that is not even considered to be a living organism. This invader is a **virus**. A virus is a nonliving particle that can reproduce only when it infects a cell. Because a virus cannot reproduce on its own, scientists do not consider it living. In addition, viruses do not share some of the other traits found in living things. For example, viruses do not grow in size and cannot absorb materials from their environment for their own use.

Viruses are so small that you need a special microscope to see them. However, despite their small size, viruses cause a number of diseases, including the common cold, flu, measles, chicken pox, pneumonia, and several STDs. No matter what disease they cause, all viruses act in the same way. A virus consists of two chemical substances. One is a protein that serves as the outer coat of the virus. The other chemical is a **nucleic acid** inside the protein coat of the virus. Nucleic acids contain the hereditary information that is passed on to future generations. Nucleic acids come in two types—**deoxyribonucleic acid** (**DNA**) and **ribonucleic acid** (**RNA**). Some viruses contain DNA; others have RNA.

When a virus attaches itself to a cell, it injects its nucleic acid while the protein coat remains outside. Inside the cell, the nucleic acid takes over the cell's "machinery." Instead of carrying out the cell's jobs, the "machinery" now produces new viruses that begin to fill up the cell. When their numbers get too large, they burst open the cell. The viruses are now set to invade and kill other cells. Several thousand viruses can be made in each infected cell, so you can imagine how quickly a viral infection spreads.

Antibiotics, of course, are useless against viruses. Viral infections are controlled in three ways. First, the immune system fights them. Second, antiviral drugs are given to an infected person. Third, vaccinations are used to prevent some viral diseases. Vaccinations have proved to be effective in eliminating certain diseases, such as smallpox. At one time, smallpox affected millions of people, killing 40 percent of its victims and leaving the remaining 60 percent scarred and often blind. A vaccination program carried out by the United Nations eliminated smallpox as a human health threat. The last case of smallpox was reported in Africa more than 20 years ago. Today, scientists are trying to develop a vaccine that would be effective against another virus, the current mass killer that causes AIDS.

## Target Organs

Now that you know the "cast of characters" that can cause STDs, we will examine the organs they target for infection. In the case of most STDs, the sex organs are the first targets. From there, the invaders can spread to other organs. The sex organs are not only primary targets of most STDs, but also the means by which the pathogen is usually passed from one person to another. To understand how this happens, we need to know more about the sex organs that are involved and examine their location in the body.

Most of a male's sex organs are actually outside the body. These organs include the **penis**, a tube-shaped organ that can become enlarged and stiff during sexual stimulation. Behind the penis lies a pouch of skin called the **scrotum**, which contains two testes. Each **testis** contains numerous, tightly coiled tubes. If the tiny tubes in both testes were spread out, they would be extend about 1,640 feet (500 meters) long. The testes produce the **sperm**—the male reproductive cells. Because they are outside the body, the testes are cooler than the temperature inside the body. Sperm need this cooler temperature to mature. When sperm are mature, they leave the testes and enter a long tube called the **urethra**. The urethra is the passageway by which both sperm and urine exit a male's body. The urethra is also the passageway into a male's body for most pathogens that cause STDs. From here, the pathogens work their way up to other parts of the body.

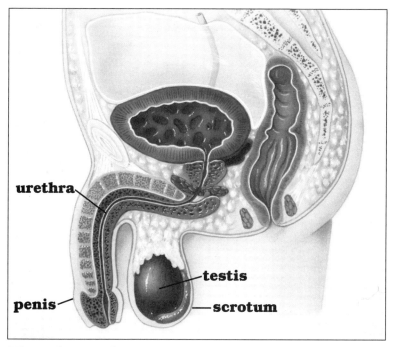

*The male reproductive system*

Unlike a male, a female's sex organs—with one exception—are inside her body. The one external female reproductive structure is the **vulva**. The vulva is made of skin and moist membranes that cover and protect the opening to the female reproductive system. That opening leads to the **vagina**, a muscular tube that is several inches long. Sperm enter a female through the vagina. The vagina connects with the **uterus**, which is commonly known as the womb. The uterus is about the size of a fist and shaped like a pear. The entrance between the vagina and the uterus is called the **cervix**. The top of the uterus connects with narrow tubes on either side of the body called **fallopian tubes**. At the top of each fallopian tube is an **ovary**, which is located inside a

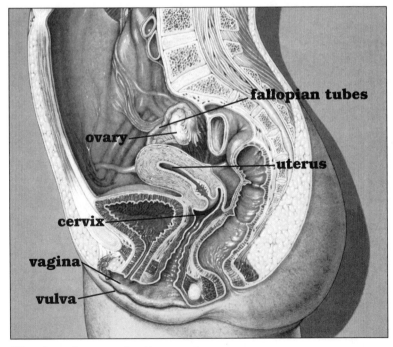

*The female reproductive system*

female's abdomen. Each ovary produces mature egg cells that travel down the fallopian tubes. A female's urethra, unlike a male's, has a separate opening to the outside. Thus eggs and urine do not follow the same route to leave the body. Pathogens that cause STDs can invade a female's body through either of these two external openings—the vagina or the urethra—and then spread to other parts of the body.

So, in both males and females, the sex organs are often the first targets for these pathogens, but not the only targets. Pathogens may grow in virtually any organ. And, in some cases, a pathogen that causes an STD may enter the body in some other way. A pathogen can enter through the mouth of a person who engages in oral sex. A pathogen can enter through the anus of a person who engages in anal sex. People who share hypodermic needles can inject a pathogen into a vein. As you can see, an invader can enter the body in several ways.

# Gonorrhea

Penicillin saved millions of soldiers' lives during World War II. But battle wounds were not the only targets of this newly discovered antibiotic. Doctors soon began treating infectious diseases of all types, including STDs, with penicillin and other antibiotic drugs. The results were equally impressive. This was especially true in the case of one particular STD—**gonorrhea**. Gonorrhea is one of the most common sexually transmitted diseases and goes by several colloquial names, including "the clap," "the drip," "a strain," "a dose," and "GC." All these names reflect the fact that gonorrhea has been a medical problem for lots of people for a very long time.

Nearly 750,000 cases of gonorrhea are reported each year in the United States. Another 750,000 cases, mostly among teenagers and young adults, are believed to be unreported each year. That makes a total of 1.5 million Americans believed to contract gonorrhea each year. Fortunately, gonorrhea can be cured quickly and completely. But, of course, only those who seek a doctor's help can be treated. Without medical treatment, the infection may spread in the body and lead to serious complications.

## Cause and Transmission

Gonorrhea is caused by a bacterium called *Neisseria gonorrheae*, named after Albert Neisser, the physician who discovered the cause of this disease in 1879. This bacterium is very delicate and can grow only in warm, moist areas of the body, especially the urethra, cervix, penis, throat, and rectum. As it turns out, the needs of this bacterium and the warm, moist living conditions in certain areas of the body are a perfect match. In fact, *Neisseria gonorrheae* infects only humans.

Like all STDs, gonorrhea is a **contagious disease**, meaning that the bacteria can be transmitted from one person to another. Gonorrhea bacteria are easily spread from person to person through physical contact, mainly as a result of sexual contact. Gonorrhea can be transmitted through vaginal, oral, or anal sex. During vaginal sex, the bacteria can be transmitted from an infected female to the urethra of the male. An infected male can transmit the bacteria to a female's urethra, but usually the bacteria invade the cervix. From here, the bacteria can spread to the uterus and the fallopian tubes. In oral sex, an infected person can transmit the bacteria to another person's throat. Anal sex allows the bacteria to enter the rectum of another person. From any one of these sites, the bacteria can spread to other parts of the body, including the eyes—because of the warm, moist environment they provide.

Transmission of gonorrhea through sexual contact is referred to as a primary contact. **Primary contact** means that an individual becomes infected by direct physical contact with an infected person. Gonorrhea can then spread through the individual's body by secondary contact. **Secondary contact** means that the bacteria are transmitted from the primary site of infection to another part of the body where they can thrive and multiply.

For example, consider what may happen in a male after gonorrhea bacteria have invaded his penis. When he touches his penis, the bacteria can rub off on his hand. If he later places his hand in his mouth, the bacteria can be passed to his throat. If he rubs his eyes, the bacteria may spread there. In either case, secondary contact allows the bacteria to spread to other parts of the body.

Transmission to other parts of the body through secondary contact can also occur in females. For example, an infected female can wipe her vulva and then touch another part of her body where the bacteria can spread. In both males and females, secondary contact occurs soon after a person touches the infected area because the bacteria cannot survive for long outside a warm, moist environment. For this reason, a person is not likely to contract gonorrhea from sitting on a toilet seat, which is a common misconception about how gonorrhea is transmitted from one person to another.

However, gonorrhea can be transmitted from an infected woman to her newborn baby during delivery. Because of this possibility, doctors recommend that a pregnant woman have at least one test for gonorrhea during her pregnancy. Most states require hospitals to administer drops in the eyes of newborn babies which contains a medication that kills gonorrhea bacteria. These drops are given to newborns just in case the mother has gonorrhea and does not know it. If the bacteria did invade the baby's eyes, the infection could lead to blindness. Over the years, this procedure has saved the sight of thousands of babies.

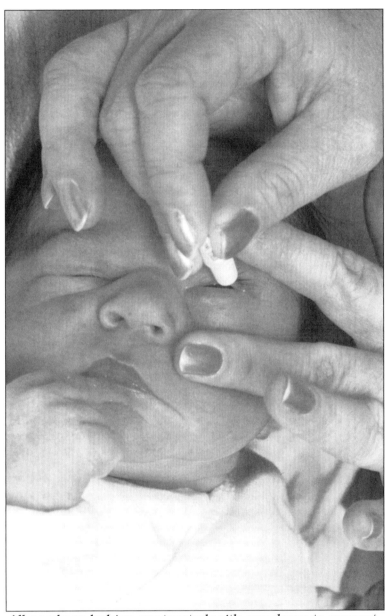

*All newborn babies are treated with eye drops to prevent any possibility that they have contracted gonorrhea from their mother.*

# Symptoms and Complications

If gonorrhea bacteria are present in the penis, some time passes before any signs or symptoms of the infection become apparent. This is known as the **incubation period**. An incubation period is the time between the moment of infection and the appearance of the first symptoms. For gonorrhea, the incubation period can be as short as two days or, in the case of males, as long as one month. Thus a person can be infected with gonorrhea bacteria and not even know it—perhaps not until a month after becoming infected. After the incubation period ends, gonorrhea affects males and females differently, depending on the body part that has been infected.

In males with gonorrhea bacteria in their penis, a thick, yellowish discharge appears in the urethra at the tip of the penis. The male has to urinate frequently, which is unfortunate because urinating is painful. At times, blood may appear in the urine. In addition, glands in the groin may become swollen. Finally, the tip of the penis may turn red because of the bacterial infection.

In the penis, the bacteria can penetrate blood vessels and then travel through the blood and infect the entire body. This condition, known as **disseminated gonorrhea**, causes fever and skin rash. The bacteria may also lodge and grow in the joints where they may cause a painful infection known as **septic arthritis**. The joints of the knees are most frequently attacked, but the bacteria may also affect the elbow and other joints in the body. If not treated, the bacteria can cause permanent damage that will affect a person's movements in the infected area. Disseminated gonorrhea and septic arthritis can also develop in infected females.

Most females who become infected with gonorrhea bacteria in their urethra or cervix have no symptoms at first. In fact, about 80 percent of women infected with gonorrhea never develop any symptoms. When symptoms do occur, they may include a redness that develops on the cervix. This change would not be obvious but it might cause pain or discomfort. Like a male, a female may have a thick, yellowish discharge, in this case from her vagina. She may also feel the urge to urinate frequently.

If no symptoms occur, or if the female chooses to ignore them, the bacteria will spread into her body and cause complications. A few days or a week after infection, the bacteria can invade the fallopian tubes, where they thrive. The fallopian tubes are only as wide as a human hair, so any swelling due to an infection can be quite significant. The swelling may cause severe pain in the lower abdomen, and a fever may develop. This condition is known as **pelvic inflammatory disease (PID)**.

As the female's body tries to fight the infection, the fallopian tubes may become swollen and filled with pus. This may cause the fallopian tubes to become blocked and scarred. If the blockage in the fallopian tubes is permanent, the female will never be able to have children of her own. Recall from Chapter 1 that an egg from an ovary passes into the fallopian tube. If sperm are present, this is where fertilization occurs. However, if the fallopian tube is blocked, fertilization is very unlikely.

Even if fertilization does occur, the egg may not be able to continue on its journey to the uterus. A fertilized egg must burrow into the wall of the uterus where it can develop for the next nine months. Blocked in the fallopian tube, the egg then tries to develop there. When a fertilized egg starts to develop in a fallopian tube, the condition is called an **ectopic pregnancy** or **tubal pregnancy**. The fallopian tube cannot support the developing baby for the entire nine months, so at some point, the fallopian tube ruptures and the pregnancy ends. The woman will then start to hemorrhage, or bleed heavily. Immediate surgery to stop the bleeding is the only way to save the woman's life.

For obvious reasons, a woman should seek medical help at the first indication that she has become infected with gonorrhea bacteria, no matter how mild the symptom may be. Even if no symptoms are present, a female who has reason to think that she may have been infected should seek immediate medical attention. A male should also get medical attention as soon as possible because gonorrhea is most easily treated in its early stages. The early stage of infection is also the time when gonorrhea is most contagious. Any physical contact with an infected person at this stage is almost certain to spread the disease to a sex partner.

Complications may also develop if the gonorrhea bacteria have invaded a site other than the sex organs. Symptoms may be even less apparent if the bacteria have invaded the throat or anus. If these areas are infected, there may be pain, itching, soreness, and a discharge of thick fluid. If the throat is infected, a person may have difficulty swallowing. If the anus is infected, the person may be constipated. But most of the time, people do not realize that their throat or anus is infected because there are no symptoms.

# Diagnosing Gonorrhea

The symptoms you have read about will make a doctor suspect that a person has gonorrhea. To be sure that the diagnosis is correct, however, the doctor will likely order two laboratory tests. Both involve taking a sample of the thickened fluid that is discharged from the penis or vagina.

One test involves use of the gram stain. The results of this test can be given to the person at the time of the visit. A sample of the discharge is placed on a slide and viewed under a microscope. But, because of their small size, bacteria are difficult to distinguish under a microscope. In addition, the sample may not contain enough bacteria to examine in detail under a microscope. Here is where the gram stain is useful. Recall from Chapter 1 that the gram stain distinguishes two types of bacteria— gram-positive and gram-negative. Gonorrhea bacteria are gram-negative. Thus if the bacteria in the discharge are gram-positive, then the person does not have gonorrhea. However, if the bacteria are gram-negative, then the person *might* have gonorrhea. Here is where the other laboratory test is important.

The second test involves placing a sample of the discharge onto a culture dish. As you read in Chapter 1, bacteria multiply rapidly. The culture dishes are incubated for two days, providing enough time for the bacteria to produce colonies. Each colony consists of millions of bacterial cells, making them easy to examine and identify under a microscope. The advantage of the culture test is that it will tell definitely if a person has gonorrhea. The disadvantage of the test is that it takes two days before the results are available. During that time, any bacteria that may be present will multiply and spread.

## Treatment and Cure

Because of the permanent damage that may occur from gonorrhea, early treatment is vital. Today, early treatment will almost certainly lead to a cure. But that was not always the case. In the past, gonorrhea was treated by squirting certain solutions into a male's urethra or a female's vagina. Various "home remedies" were also used in this way to treat gonorrhea. No matter what was used, the procedure was not only uncomfortable but also ineffective. Even today some people continue to believe that these solutions will cure gonorrhea and that there is no need to see a doctor. Anyone who follows such a treatment procedure in the hope of curing his or her gonorrhea is facing serious and permanent damage to their health.

The only effective treatment for gonorrhea is an antibiotic. When penicillin was first discovered, a single injection containing a large dose of the antibiotic cured gonorrhea overnight in 99 percent of the cases. But that success rate did not last forever. In Chapter 1 you read about the growing number of bacteria that have become resistant to antibiotics. This includes the gonorrhea bacteria. Doctors soon discovered that penicillin was becoming less and less effective in treating gonorrhea. In some cases, the antibiotic did not work at all.

When penicillin began to fail, other antibiotics had to be used. At first, doctors prescribed tetracycline. But gonorrhea soon became resistant to this antibiotic, too. As resistance to antibiotics increased, scientists had to develop an "army" of antibiotics that would be effective against gonorrhea. If one proves ineffective, another can be used. Today, doctors have several antibiotics at their disposal to treat gonorrhea. These antibiotics are taken in either pill form or by injection.

Like penicillin, a single dose of a recently developed antibiotic can cure gonorrhea in its early stages. Treating gonorrhea with this antibiotic can be done in a medical clinic where the professional staff can monitor how well the patient cooperates and responds. This type of treatment is referred to as DOT (Directly Observed Therapy). On the negative side, any antibiotic used to treat gonorrhea may cause nausea, diarrhea, abdominal pain, or dizziness. However, considering what might happen if gonorrhea is left untreated, these side effects are a small price to pay.

No matter what antibiotic is prescribed, it is extremely important that it be taken exactly as the doctor directs. Many people stop taking the antibiotic as soon as they start feeling better. If this is done, the infection will likely reappear within a week. A person must be sure to take the antibiotic as long as the doctor has prescribed and not just until the symptoms begin to disappear. Proper treatment will also prevent resistant bacteria from establishing themselves in the body. If the antibiotic is not taken as directed, the body's immune system will have to fight both sensitive and resistant bacteria. However, when the antibiotic is taken as directed, the immune system can focus on the resistant bacteria and leave the sensitive bacteria to be destroyed by the antibiotic.

In overcoming an invader, the immune system normally develops a "memory." Each time it comes across the same invader, the immune system attacks it more quickly. Thus the invader has less opportunity to spread through the body and cause serious complications. In the case of gonorrhea bacteria, however, the immune system's "memory" is not highly effective. For this reason, many people acquire gonorrhea more than once. With each infection, a person must start from "square one" and begin all over with the treatment. Two people who frequently have sex together can reinfect each other time and again unless both are treated and cured at the same time to break this reinfection cycle. To avoid reinfection and possible transmission to others, neither of them should have any sexual contact with anyone until they are cured. Such people also have other responsibilities and obligations.

## Steps to Take

Anyone who thinks they have gonorrhea should speak with either a family or clinic doctor as soon as possible. Prompt medical attention is important both to avoid complications and to prevent the disease from being passed on to others. All doctors are familiar with gonorrhea, including its cause, symptoms, and treatment. In most cases, a family doctor—a person who is known and trusted—is the best choice when seeking medical attention for gonorrhea or any STD. A concern that arises when seeing the family doctor is confidentiality. Medical ethics prevent a doctor from providing anyone, including parents, with information that was given in confidence. Teenagers should not worry about what might happen if they test positive for gonorrhea because such information should remain confidential. Instead they should worry about what might happen if they do not seek medical attention.

Teenagers, however, are often reluctant to seek medical attention when they suspect they have an STD such as gonorrhea. A typical feeling can be seen in such expressions as "If my father knew that I was sexually active, he would kill me," or "This is something that I can't talk about to anyone." As a result of such feelings, gonorrhea and other STDs are spreading rapidly among teenagers. To eliminate concerns about confidentiality, the person should first talk with the family doctor about the importance of privacy. The person should make it very clear that any information or health records must not be shared with anyone else unless permission is given. This understanding should be reached before any medical condition or concerns are discussed. If the doctor is unwilling to respect the person's confidentiality, or if the person is not sure of the doctor's position, then the person should find another doctor, perhaps at a medical clinic.

Because STDs are widely recognized as a public health menace, every community has a hospital or clinic with staff members who are knowledgeable about these diseases. A person can seek medical attention at one of these facilities with the understanding that their confidentiality will be respected. For help in locating a clinic where gonorrhea can be treated, a person can look in the telephone book for the number of their local Public Health Department facility. If money is a concern, STD clinics will provide diagnostic and treatment services at no cost to the patient.

Even when a trusted family doctor is available, some people feel more comfortable in seeking medical attention from a hospital or clinic where they feel that their condition will be kept confidential. The point is that *where* a person infected with gonorrhea seeks medical help is not important. What *is* important is simply getting the help, especially at the first indication of a gonorrhea infection. What is just as important is to be sure that any sex partners are also examined for signs of possible infection. Thus an infected person will be asked to identify, if possible, the person from whom they caught the infection and, in turn, any persons to whom they may have spread the bacteria.

A person's responsibility is not only to seek medical attention to treat his or her gonorrhea, but also to try to prevent its spread to someone else. Because gonorrhea is highly contagious and may not cause any symptoms, a person who has sexual contact with more than one partner should be tested regularly for the disease. "Safe sex" is also recommended to prevent the spread of not only gonorrhea but also any other STD. Measures that can be taken to prevent the spread of STDs will be described in Chapter 9.

# 3 Syphilis

One of the oldest known STDs is **syphilis**. Syphilis has an interesting history that dates back to the ancient Greeks. Syphilis got its name from the story of a mythological Greek shepherd named Syphilus. According to the myth, Syphilus was stricken with this horrible disease as a punishment for having insulted the god Apollo. The disease itself first appeared in Europe quite suddenly in the late 1400s or early 1500s. No one knows exactly where in Europe syphilis started, but the disease was greatly feared because anyone who became infected was likely to experience a painful and horrible death. Even doctors at that time were so terrified of syphilis that they would not even write down its name. Instead, they used the Greek letter sigma ($\Sigma$) as a symbol for syphilis. Even today some medical students write $\Sigma$ in their notes as a shorthand for syphilis.

After making its appearance in Europe, syphilis spread throughout the continent within a matter of a few decades. At the time, Europe was racked by incessant wars. Undoubtedly, syphilis was carried far and wide by armies of soldiers and their camp followers as they marched across Europe. No country wanted the distinction of being the site where syphilis first appeared. Thus Italian soldiers called syphilis the "French Disease," while French soldiers called it the "Spanish Disease." Naturally, Spanish soldiers passed the blame on to others.

Some historians believe that syphilis actually originated in the New World, perhaps among Native Americans in the Caribbean and Mexico. The voyages of Christopher Columbus may have been responsible for spreading syphilis to Europe. His voyages occurred just a short time before the disease appeared in Europe. Spanish explorers on these voyages may have contracted the disease in the New World and brought it to Europe when they returned home. Some historians believe syphilis was a mild and relatively harmless disease when it first appeared. But at some point, the nature of the disease changed dramatically. Suddenly, syphilis became a dreaded killer.

Shortly after being infected, victims developed raging fevers and open sores on the skin. Syphilis was a swift and terrible killer, causing death within the first few days of infection in many cases. For those who survived, the disease spread quickly, invading the heart, eyes, brains, bones, and almost every other part of the body. Most of those who had survived the first few days died within weeks. The overall death rate from the disease at that time was very high. Historians estimate that nearly 10 million Europeans died of syphilis during its first outbreak in the late 1400s or early 1500s.

Syphilis continued to pose a threat through the centuries as it spread from Europe to areas all over the world. Once infected, victims passed through various stages of the disease. Syphilis now took its time in claiming its victims. The final stage of the disease might not occur for years or even decades after the initial infection. During that time, the pathogen that causes syphilis invaded nearly every organ in the body. Vital organs, such as the heart, eyes, bones, nerves, and brain became infected. The victim might develop heart disease, blindness, physical disabilities, paralysis, and mental illness. Because the symptoms that appear at this last stage mimic or imitate symptoms of many other diseases, syphilis has been referred to as the "Great Imitator." In the end, the "Great Imitator" often proved fatal.

## An Unethical Study

In the 1930s, syphilis was the focus of a study conducted at the Tuskegee Institute in Alabama. The United States Public Health Service (PHS) was trying to learn more about syphilis, looking especially for an effective treatment. The site in Alabama was chosen because a survey had revealed that between 35 and 40 percent of all age groups in the area had tested positive for syphilis. At that time, doctors were not sure whether syphilis affected people of different races in the same way. The population in the Alabama site was 80 percent African-American, making it ideally suited for a study on how syphilis affected this particular race. The study involved 600 African American men—399 with syphilis and 201 who did not have the disease. The study was called the "Tuskegee Study of Untreated Syphilis in the Negro Male." The Tuskegee study began in 1932 and was supposed to last six months. It wound up continuing for 40 years, finally ending in 1972 when its true nature was reported in the newspapers.

As you can tell from the name of the study, doctors made no attempt to treat the men with syphilis, even though an effective treatment was discovered in the 1940s. The men were told only that they were being treated for "bad blood," a general term that could be used to describe any one of several medical conditions. But in fact, the men were not actually treated for any medical problem, including those men who had syphilis. All the men received during the entire study was something that doctors called "pink medicine." This medication consisted of nothing more than aspirin dissolved in a colored solution. Because none of the men in the study had ever taken aspirin, they felt that it would cure whatever they had.

In return for taking part in the study, the men received free medical exams. But those who tested positive for syphilis were never told that they had the disease. All the men in the study also received free meals on the days they were examined. In addition, they were given transportation to the clinic and were provided with free medical care for any minor problems. Another benefit given to the men could be considered an omen—a free $50 burial.

Throughout the study, doctors not only withheld proper medical treatment from those with syphilis, but they also prevented other agencies from providing medical care. During World War II, about 50 men in the study were drafted into the army. Like anyone else entering the army, those with syphilis were ordered to undergo the treatment available at the time. But the PHS forced the draft boards to deny treatment to the men from the Tuskegee study. At the same time, the PHS was providing treatment to people with syphilis in other parts of the United States. But they again excluded the Tuskegee men. For the next 30 years, the PHS continued to prevent the men from getting proper medical attention. The PHS even kept track of those who left Alabama during the course of the study. Local health departments where the men moved were told not to treat the men. Over the course of the study, more than 100 men died of syphilis. Most, if not all, could have been saved with the proper treatment that was available at the time.

In the 1960s, a PHS worker heard about the Tuskegee study. Concerned about the lack of medical treatment for the men, he attempted to make changes in the project. But his efforts were unsuccessful. Finally, the worker provided information to a Washington, D.C. newspaper, which broke the story on July 25, 1972—40 years after the Tuskegee study started! The public was outraged about how the men had been treated. In response to public concerns, the study was finally disbanded. But the damage had been done. Even those who had survived the disease suffered from horrible syphilis-related conditions that may have contributed to their later deaths.

One year after the study was ended, a civil rights lawyer brought a $1.8-billion suit against the institutions and individuals involved in the Tuskegee study. The suit sought $3 million for each living participant and for the heirs of each man who had died. The case never came to trial. In 1974, the year after the suit was filed, the federal government agreed to an out-of-court settlement of $10 million. Each survivor received $37,500. The heirs of each survivor got only $15,000 that was to be divided among all of them. The lawyer who filed the civil rights suit was payed $1 million for his efforts. Once again, people felt that the Tuskegee men and their families were the victims.

No one involved in the study ever apologized to the survivors or the families of those who died of syphilis. No one ever thought the PHS was doing something wrong or immoral. In fact, the PHS directors felt that they were acting in good conscience. Other saw it differently. They felt that the study was racist—all the PHS directors were white while all the subjects were black. This sentiment was shared by President Bill Clinton, who finally offered an apology on behalf of the federal government to the families of the men in the Tuskegee study. His apology was made in 1997—65 years after the Tuskegee study had begun.

*At a news conference, President Bill Clinton and Vice President Al Gore, with one of the victims of the Tuskegee syphilis study, make a formal apology on behalf of the U.S. government for the racist experiment.*

# Cause and Transmission

Like gonorrhea, syphilis is caused by a bacterium. The bacterium responsible for syphilis is called *Treponema pallidum*, which has an unusual shape.

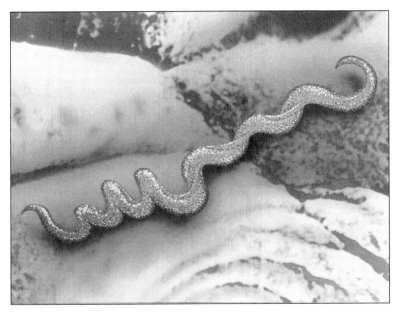

*The bacterium that causes syphilis, Treponema pallidum, has a corkscrew shape.*

Like the bacterium that causes gonorrhea, *Treponema pallidum* is delicate and requires a warm, moist environment to survive. Once again, the human body provides an ideal place in which this bacterium can thrive and multiply.

The bacterium can invade the body without any break in the skin. Syphilis is transmitted from one person to another through direct physical contact, usually during vaginal, oral, or anal sex. Syphilis can also be transmitted by kissing. All that is needed is for a person to come in direct contact with a syphilis sore, known as a **chancre**. Because the bacterium cannot survive outside a warm, moist environment, syphilis cannot be transmitted through toilet seats, door knobs, swimming pools, hot tubs, or eating utensils.

Like gonorrhea, syphilis can be transmitted from a pregnant woman to her unborn child, especially if the mother is not being treated for the disease. About 25 percent of these pregnancies result in a stillbirth—a baby who is born dead. Those who live will probably have syphilis at birth, a condition known as **congenital syphilis**. A baby with congenital syphilis may not show any symptoms, or they may go undetected for as long as three months. Symptoms may include skin chancres, rashes, fever, yellowish skin, and a swollen liver. Care must be taken when handling a baby with syphilis because the chancres are infectious. If not treated, as infected babies become children and teenagers, they may develop problems with their teeth, eyes, ears, bones, and brain because of the damage done by syphilis bacteria.

## Stages of Syphilis

The incubation period for syphilis is anywhere from 10 to 90 days, with an average of 21 days. During this time, bacteria that have invaded the penis, vulva, mouth, or rectum begin to spread. In the penis and vulva, the bacteria grow just beneath the skin. The first symptom of an infection is the appearance of a chancre. This small, painless sore usually forms on the penis, vulva, or even inside the vagina. As a result of oral sex or kissing, a chancre can also form inside the mouth. One or more chancres may appear following infection with syphilis bacteria. The appearance of a chancre marks the first stage of syphilis. Because the chancre is small and painless, a person may not even notice it. Despite its small size however, the chancre is teeming with syphilis bacteria. As a result, syphilis is very contagious and easily transmitted to another person during this first stage.

The first stage of syphilis does not last long—anywhere from one to six weeks. During this time, a chancre may ooze a clear liquid filled with syphilis bacteria. Direct contact with this fluid will result in a case of syphilis. Gradually, the chancre heals itself, but looks are deceiving. Although the chancre has disappeared, the bacteria are still present in the body. The bacteria enter the bloodstream and travel to other parts of the body, bringing about the second stage of syphilis.

The second stage begins when one or more areas of the skin develop a non-itching rash. In addition, a person may develop a fever, headache, sore throat, and a general feeling of fatigue. The rash may cover the whole body, or it may develop in just a few areas, such as the palms of the hands or the soles of the feet. The rash can take any one of several appearances. In some cases, the rash is barely noticeable. In addition, not everyone who becomes infected with syphilis bacteria develops a rash. Those who do develop a noticeable rash can seek immediate medical attention. Those who do not get a rash often go untreated.

The rash can last from two to six weeks, and, like a chancre, it can heal on its own. Despite the lack of any symptoms at the end of the second stage, an infected person is still highly contagious and can pass along the bacteria to anyone by sexual contact. The person may remain in this second stage for as long as one to two years after the initial infection. During that time, the symptoms of syphilis, including the rash, may come and go. If left untreated, syphilis will progress to the next stage of the disease.

Following the second stage, infected individuals enter the latent or "silent" stage, which can last for months or even years. Despite not being treated, many people will not suffer any consequences of syphilis during the latent stage. During this time, the person has no symptoms of the disease. A latent stage can also occur between the first and second stages. Soon after the initial infection and throughout the latent period, a person's immune system is attacking the syphilis bacteria. The immune system will be successful in about 70 percent of those who have been infected. The remaining 30 percent will go on to the third stage of syphilis.

The third stage can reveal itself in many ways. At this stage, syphilis bacteria can attack the heart, brain, bones, liver, and any other organ in the body. The third stage may begin as soon as one year following the initial infection or as long as 20 years later. If the syphilis bacteria attack the heart or blood vessels, the condition is known as **cardiovascular syphilis**. The bacteria can affect the **aorta**, the major artery that carries blood from the heart. The infection can cause the aorta to swell or balloon, producing a condition called an **aneurysm**. The aorta may burst, causing instant death.

If the bacteria invade the brain, the result is a condition known as **neurosyphilis**. Some people with neurosyphilis never develop any symptoms. Other people with neurosyphilis may get a headache, stiff neck, or a fever that results from an inflammation of the lining of the brain where the bacteria have produced an infection. Still others may experience seizures, numbness, weakness, and problems seeing. Syphilis is rightly named the "Great Imitator" for all the symptoms that can appear during the third stage.

## Diagnosing Syphilis

A person should suspect syphilis if a chancre appears on a sex organ (the first stage of the disease) or if a completely unexplained skin rash appears anywhere on the body (the second stage of the disease). In either case, immediate medical attention should be sought. A doctor will take a sample from either the chancre or the rash for examination under a microscope. The syphilis bacteria do not readily absorb a stain, which makes identification

*A scientist can use an electron microscope to take a close look at bacteria, including those that cause syphilis.*

difficult. A laboratory technician who is well trained in identifying the bacteria is usually called upon to make the diagnosis. The technician will use a special microscope but even then, the bacteria are often not found. Of course, if there is no chancre or rash to provide a sample for observation, the bacteria will never be found. Fortunately, there is another procedure that can be done to test for syphilis.

This procedure is a blood test. Actually, several blood tests can diagnose syphilis. These tests detect the proteins made by a person's immune system to fight the syphilis bacteria. Starting about 10 days after the initial infection, the body's immune system begins to react against the syphilis bacteria. Specialized white blood cells release a protein known as an **antibody**. An antibody is a protein that is made by a white blood cell in response to anything foreign, especially a pathogen, that invades the body. As you read in Chapter 1, a chemical secreted by white blood cells clumps pathogens, making it easier for other white blood cells to destroy them. This chemical is an antibody. Each invader provokes the production of a different antibody. Thus, if syphilis bacteria have invaded the body, antibodies that are specific for this pathogen should be present. The more pathogens that have invaded the body or the longer they have been present, the more antibodies will be present in the bloodstream.

These antibodies serve two purposes. First, they can be used to diagnose syphilis. The blood test for syphilis uses chemicals that can detect any antibodies the body may have produced to destroy syphilis bacteria. The test is so simple and inexpensive that doctors usually order it whenever a person has a complete physical examination. At one time, most U.S. states required a blood test for syphilis before a marriage license could be issued. This requirement has been discontinued in most states, but doctors still recommend it as a precaution for people who are about to get married. Anyone who has a positive test result can then get immediate medical attention to prevent syphilis from advancing to its next stage.

A blood test for syphilis, however, is not 100 percent reliable. During the first six weeks after the initial infection, there may not be enough antibodies in the blood to be detected. The result will then be a false negative—the test does not reveal that the person is infected with syphilis bacteria. On the other hand, the blood test can at times give a false positive result, especially in older people. In this case, the test would indicate that the person has syphilis, when in reality the person does not have the disease.

The second purpose served by the antibodies is an indication that the body is mounting an attack against the disease. Recall that about 70 percent of individuals infected with syphilis bacteria do not go past the second stage. Many are diagnosed with the disease and receive the proper medical care. Others are never diagnosed as having syphilis. But fortunately their immune systems are successful in preventing the disease from advancing to the third stage. The bacteria are either destroyed all at once or slowly during the second stage of the disease. Thus these people are cured without any medical treatment and remain free of the syphilis bacteria, unless they are foolish enough to get reinfected. Reinfection is possible because the immune system does not create a "memory" that serves to destroy any syphilis bacteria as soon as they again invade the body.

# Treatment

Before the early 1940s, syphilis was a very difficult disease to treat. The best treatment available at the time was a long, painful procedure that involved the use of heavy metals. These metals are poisonous and produce unpleasant side effects. One metal that was used to treat syphilis was arsenic. The benefit of arsenic was actually an accidental discovery. In 1910, a German scientist named Paul Ehrlich was looking for a way to treat a disease called African sleeping sickness. Ehrlich came up with a substance he called salvarsan-606, a name he chose because it was the 606th treatment he had tested. The treatment did not work for African sleeping sickness, but it was found to be effective against syphilis. Salvarsan-606 could cure syphilis, but it worked slowly and was very toxic. However, it was the only treatment available until antibiotics were discovered.

Today, syphilis is treated with penicillin, which is usually given by injection. Other antibiotics are

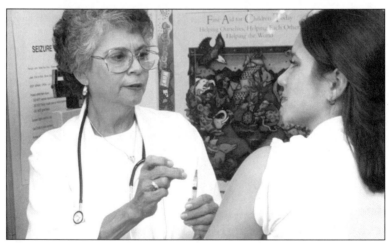

*A single injection of penicillin is the usual treatment for syphilis.*

also effective if the person is allergic to penicillin. One large dose is usually all that is needed to cure a syphilis infection. But there is a downside to the treatment. Over 50 percent of people with syphilis in either the first or second stage have side effects within 6 to 12 hours after taking the antibiotic. They may develop a fever, headaches, sweating, chills, and a temporary worsening of their chancres or skin rash. Those who experience the reaction often feel that their condition is getting worse, even though their doctor probably warned them about the side effects. The side effects last for only about 24 hours and leave no permanent marks.

Fortunately, syphilis bacteria have not developed a resistance to penicillin. People who are being treated for syphilis should have a periodic blood test to check that the syphilis bacteria have been completely destroyed. Persons with neurosyphilis may have to be tested for two years after treatment begins. Although syphilis may be cured, any damage that has been done by the bacteria cannot be undone.

## The Continuing Epidemic

If syphilis can be cured so easily, then why is it still a major health problem? Actually, syphilis is a health concern in only certain cities in the United States. For example, in 1996 only one new case of syphilis was reported in Seattle, Washington. But during the first six months of 1999, the city recorded 13 new cases of syphilis, following 25 cases reported in 1998. Other major cities, including New York, Boston, and San Francisco reported similar increases in the spread of syphilis in 1999. For most of the country, however, the disease peaked in 1990 when 200 of every 100,000 people in the population were infected. The latest reports show a decline in that rate. But syphilis still remains a major health problem for many reasons.

First, syphilis is difficult to diagnose, especially in the early stages. If syphilis is not detected, it cannot be treated and cured. Second, people can be reinfected a number of times because the immune system does not have a "memory" against the disease. Third, the strength or **virulence** of syphilis bacteria varies over time. Recall that when syphilis first appeared in Europe in the late 1400s or early 1500s, it was usually fatal. In the 1920s and 1930s also, the bacteria killed a lot of people in the United States. This was followed by a period when the bacteria were not quite as deadly. Finally, and perhaps most important, syphilis is still a major health problem because those likely to get it—sexually active young people—do not take the necessary precautions. As you will see in Chapter 9, preventing syphilis, or any STD, is not hard.

# 4 Herpes

Something was definitely wrong. It started with his hips. At first it was just an ache, perhaps from all the swimming he was doing that summer at the beach. Because he did not think it was anything serious, he decided not to mention the ache to his parents. But one day the ache turned into a pain that bothered him when he walked. Still he decided not to say anything to his parents because he felt the pain would disappear if he simply rested his legs for a few days. The next day, however, he realized that the situation was worse than he had thought. A small cluster of painful, itchy blisters appeared on his penis. Greg knew then that he had to speak with his parents.

Greg's father suspected that something serious was wrong with his son and decided to take him to a doctor immediately. After performing an examination and getting the results of a lab test, the doctor told Greg, who was only 16 at the time, that he had an STD called **genital herpes**. Genital herpes affects approximately 25 million people in the United States alone and countless millions in the rest of the world. About 500,000 new cases occur each year just in the United States. That summer, Greg was one of those 500,000 people.

When Greg was informed that genital herpes is sexually transmitted, he thought back to what had happened a few weeks earlier. He and a few friends had been hanging out one night on the boardwalk where they met some girls. Everyone decided to have a beach party that lasted all night. They began drinking and soon Greg was having sex with a girl he had just met. Greg never saw her again after the next morning, but he would always have something that would remind him of her—genital herpes.

The doctor gave Greg an ointment to apply to the blisters on his penis. The medicine helped, and the blisters healed, but not permanently. Several weeks later, the blisters reappeared on Greg's penis. This time, the doctor prescribed an oral medication that was more likely to keep Greg's condition under control, but was also much more expensive. The pills proved to be more effective than the ointment in preventing the blisters from forming. But Greg was aware that he could get the painful blisters at any time for the rest of his life because genital herpes can never be cured. Whenever the blisters were present, Greg was warned not to be sexually active because he would transmit genital herpes to his sex partner. All of Greg's problems could have been avoided if he had only known the facts about genital herpes.

Not too long ago most people knew little, if anything, about genital herpes, primarily because no one talked about it much. If anyone had this disease, they were too embarrassed to admit it, much less talk about it. Even doctors did not know much about the pathogen that causes genital herpes. All this has changed. Today, almost everyone has heard about genital herpes, and doctors know about the pathogen responsible for this STD. Because genital herpes is spreading rapidly among sexually active teenagers and young adults, knowledge of genital herpes is more important than ever.

# Cause and Transmission

Genital herpes is caused by a virus known as **herpes simplex**. The herpes simplex virus is similar to the viruses that cause chicken pox and infectious mononucleosis. As you read in Chapter 1, viruses are so small that they can be seen only with the help of an electron microscope. The herpes simplex virus actually exists in two different strains because of the way they act in the human body. One strain, designated **herpes simplex virus type 1**, generally attacks the mouth region. This strain causes blisters known as "cold sores" or "fever blisters." These cold sores may form on the lips and inside the mouth.

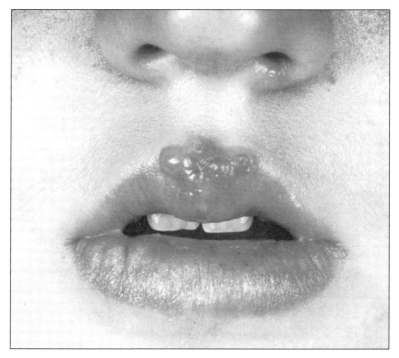

*A cluster of blisters on the upper lip is characteristic of the herpes simplex virus.*

Once it has successfully invaded a person's body, the herpes type 1 virus never leaves. Most of the time, it remains inactive and does no damage. A number of factors, especially emotional stress, may cause the virus to become active and produce cold sores. Other factors that can activate the herpes virus include sunlight, sexual activity, and an illness such as the flu or a cold. When it is not active, the virus hides in nerve cells located in the lower jaw. Under the right conditions, the virus leaves the nerve cells and travels to the mouth region where it usually causes cold sores to form. The virus can be transmitted to another person by direct contact with the sore through touching, kissing, or rubbing. After several days, the virus again returns to its hiding place in the nerve cells where it is able to escape destruction by the immune system.

Greg's problems were caused by a close relative of the virus that produces cold sores. Genital herpes is most often caused by **herpes simplex virus type 2**. This virus produces blisters on the sex organs, or **genitals**. But the word "genital" in genital herpes refers only to the area that is infected and not to the type of virus that caused the infection. For example, a person with cold sores may transmit herpes type 1 virus to a sex partner during oral sex. The sex partner may then develop genital herpes that becomes evident on his penis or her vulva. In such a situation, the sex partner has developed type 1 genital herpes. Most often, however, people with genital herpes have the type 2 virus that has been acquired through vaginal, oral, or anal sex.

Like herpes simplex type 1, the type 2 virus never leaves the body. When the virus is not active, it hides in nerve cells along the lower spinal cord.

At this point, the virus is said to be in its latent or dormant phase. The virus can become active at any time, however. Various factors can cause the type 2 virus to enter its active phase and travel back down the spinal cord to infect the penis or vulva. On average, a person infected with the herpes type 2 virus may experience between four and seven recurrences a year. Recurrences tend to be less frequent in those infected with the type 1 virus. Applying medication at the first indication that the herpes virus is becoming active may prevent a full-scale outbreak. Signs that the virus may be becoming active include tenderness, numbness, or itching in the area that it usually attacks. As a person gets older, the outbreaks become less frequent and less severe.

## Herpes Infections and Episodes

As mentioned earlier, herpes simplex virus is spreading rapidly. Between 50 and 90 percent of adults have been infected with the type 1 virus. Infections in children are often mild or cause no symptoms at all. Because of differences in the two types of viruses, the immune system is not forewarned about a type 2 virus infection after experiencing a type 1 virus infection. That means a person who has been infected with the type 1 virus can still become infected with the type 2 virus.

The first reaction to a type 2 virus infection may go unnoticed, be very mild, or be quite uncomfortable and painful. Because of this wide variation in the symptoms it may—or may not— produce, genital herpes is not diagnosed as often as it should be. As few as 20 percent of the people infected with the type 2 virus are diagnosed properly. Another 20 percent may not have any symptoms and therefore go undiagnosed. The remaining 60 percent of the people infected with the type 2 virus may be misdiagnosed. A doctor may think blisters that form in areas other than the genitals are not indicative of genital herpes. However, the type 2 virus can cause blisters to form on the buttocks, lower back, or even on the thighs. Doctors are advised to consider any blisters that appear below the waist as a sign of genital herpes.

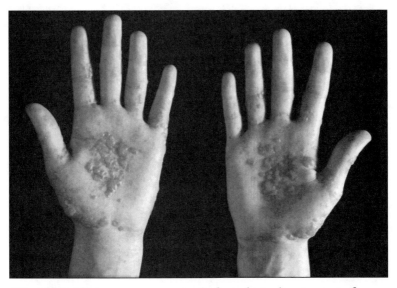

*Wart-like blisters on a person's hands indicate an infection caused by the herpes simplex virus.*

Because of the complex nature of the herpes simplex virus, doctors distinguish between the first time a person becomes infected with the virus and the first time a person experiences a reaction to the virus by developing obvious symptoms. The first time a person becomes infected is known as the **primary infection**, which may not produce any symptoms. For example, consider what may happen when a parent or some other relative kisses a baby. If the parent or relative had a cold sore at the time, the baby may become infected with the type 1 virus. Chances are no one would know that the baby had been infected because symptoms rarely appear. But the kiss would have been responsible for the primary infection.

Now consider what may happen when the baby becomes a teenager or young adult and has sex with someone who has active genital herpes. The person may again become infected with herpes virus, this time the type 2 virus. Recall that this is not the person's first infection with the herpes virus. But this may be the person's first visible reaction to an infection caused by a herpes virus. The person may first notice a dull ache in the hips, lower back, or legs for a day or so and may develop a slight fever. Then one or more clusters of small, red, itchy pimples may appear on or around the sex organs. Most often these pimples show up on the soft, moist folds of the vulva or on the skin of the penis. But, as mentioned earlier, blisters can appear on other parts of the body that come in direct contact with the virus. At first, the pimples only itch. But they soon begin to ache and burn. Within a day or so, the pimples change into fluid-filled blisters called **vesicles**. When these vesicles break open, they leave raw, painful, open sores.

This is the time when an infected person is most contagious. A broken vesicle releases millions of viruses that can infect another person who comes in direct contact with them, especially as a result of sexual activity. This period will last from two to three weeks and is known as the **first episode** with genital herpes. The first episode may be relatively mild or it can be quite severe, depending on whether the person has been exposed to the herpes virus earlier in life. For the baby who acquired a first infection with the type 1 virus through a kiss, the first episode may be mild. In this case, the baby's immune system had developed a "memory" to some extent and was able to prevent a full-scale outbreak of the infection. But if a person has never been exposed to the herpes virus, then the first episode can be severe. In other words, if the first episode occurs at the same time as the first infection, then a person may experience many, if not all, of the symptoms associated with genital herpes.

In addition to the blisters that form on the genitals, a person may find it uncomfortable or even painful to urinate. Glands in the groin region may be tender and swollen. A person may also develop flu-like symptoms, including muscle aches and pains, or possibly a fever and headaches. Females may experience a discharge from the vagina. These symptoms usually clear up completely within two to three weeks, and much sooner if the infection is treated. Several factors affect how severe the symptoms are during this time. Recall that one factor is whether or not the person had been previously infected by the herpes virus but did not develop any symptoms. Other factors include how many viruses infected the body, the condition of the person's immune system at the time, and the virulence of the herpes strain.

The disappearance of all symptoms means that the herpes virus has taken up residence in the nerve cells where it enters its latent phase. At this point, the disease is no longer contagious as the infected person cannot pass the virus to someone else. About 10 to 15 percent of the people who become infected with herpes virus never experience another episode of the disease. In effect, the virus remains permanently in its latent phase. But for everyone else who has been infected, the virus can become active at any time. This results in a **recurrent episode**.

## Recurrent Episodes

Any reappearance of the symptoms of a herpes virus infection after the first episode is known as a recurrent episode. Recurrent episodes occur more frequently with herpes type 2 virus than with the type 1 virus. Recurrent episodes, like first episodes, are highly variable. Usually the symptoms are less severe than those experienced during a primary episode. In fact, the person may not even be aware that the disease has once again become active. If symptoms do develop, they probably include blisters that usually form in about the same places as they did in the earlier episode. They may not hurt as much, and they may last only a few days this time before healing. But these blisters are as dangerous as the first ones— when they break open, viruses are released that can infect another person. So, whenever blisters are present, a person infected with herpes should not come in direct contact with another person, and especially not engage in any form of sexual activity. It is also wise to avoid sharing any article that has come in contact with a blister. For example, a wet towel or razor that has been used on an infected area may serve as a vehicle for transmitting genital herpes.

## Diagnosing Herpes

Herpes can be diagnosed with a culture test. It takes one to three days before results are available. A sample of fluid is taken from a vesicle and cultured in the laboratory. If the herpes virus is present in the sample, it will grow in the culture. The culture test also distinguishes between the two types of herpes virus. If the culture test is positive, no further testing is required. Treatment can then begin to eliminate the infection. However, a negative culture test does not necessarily mean that the person is free of the herpes virus. A negative result may be obtained if the sample is taken too long after the vesicles had first appeared. In that case, the viruses may have already retreated to take refuge in nerve cells. If the culture test is negative, blood tests are available to ensure that a person has not been infected with herpes.

A doctor will be most careful in making a diagnosis when it comes to a pregnant woman. If the woman has active genital herpes at the time her baby is born, there is a good chance that the baby may contract the virus during delivery. The chance of transmitting herpes to a newborn is greater if the mother is experiencing a primary episode rather than a recurrent episode. When a woman has a primary episode, her baby has a 50 percent chance of acquiring the herpes virus during delivery. Most of these deliveries result in a miscarriage, premature labor, or retarded growth of the newborn. Because a newborn's immune system is barely functioning, a herpes infection may even result in death.

If a pregnant woman is having a recurrent episode, then the chance of her baby acquiring the herpes virus drops to 5 percent or less. However, a pregnant woman with a history of herpes infections must be watched very closely as the time of her delivery nears. If her infection recurs and symptoms appear, doctors may decide to perform a cesarean section. In this procedure, the baby is delivered through an incision made in the abdomen. In that way, the baby will not pass through the vagina where it could come in contact with the virus in vesicles that may be present. A cesarean delivery may also be performed if a woman is experiencing a primary episode.

The danger is clear if a pregnant woman is experiencing an episode—symptoms of a herpes infection are obvious. But the real danger of acquiring a herpes infection is that the virus is usually transmitted when a person shows no symptoms, which is often the case in both primary and recurrent infections. Consequently, the vast majority of people who have herpes do not know they are infected. Approximately 75 percent of these people are believed to engage in some form of sexual activity that can transmit the disease to another person. This includes fathers-to-be. A mother-to-be can thus become infected without even knowing it by acquiring the virus from her husband. Studies have shown that 70 percent of women who had babies born with herpes had no symptoms of the disease at the time of delivery. Doctors have yet to develop an effective way to protect babies from these symptomless infections, which can be quite extensive.

Doctors are also concerned about the future health of a woman with herpes, even if she never gets pregnant. Women with herpes get cancer of the cervix about five times more often than other women. This does not mean that the herpes virus causes cancer. In fact, scientists suspect that another virus may actually be the cause of cervical cancer. The connection between the herpes virus and cervical cancer remains a mystery, but fortunately, early signs of cervical cancer are easy to detect with a test known as a **Pap smear**. Because cervical cancer is highly curable if detected early, a Pap smear is recommended once a year for all women, whether they have herpes or not.

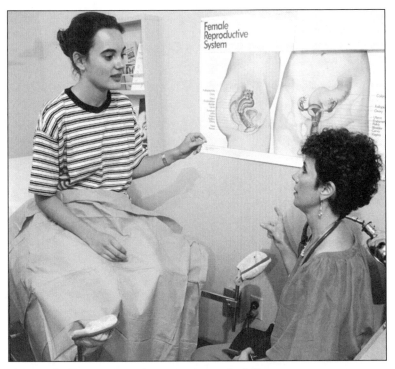

*A yearly Pap smear is recommended for young women whether or not they are sexually active.*

## Treatment

Until about 15 years ago, there was no way to treat a herpes infection. As we discussed in Chapter 1, antibiotics are effective against bacteria and have no impact on viruses. A person experiencing a herpes episode just had to wait until his or her immune system destroyed the viruses. Today, the news is different. Doctors can prescribe one of several drugs that inhibit the activity of the herpes virus. Such drugs are known as **antiviral drugs**.

The first antiviral drug used to treat a herpes infection was acyclovir, available under the trade name Zovirax. Acyclovir does not kill herpes viruses so it cannot cure a person. But the antiviral drug prevents the virus from reproducing, so it shortens the time it takes for sores and blisters to heal by limiting the number of viruses that are produced. At first, the drug was applied to the infected area as an ointment. Later, the drug became available in pill form for people who suffer severe, recurrent episodes of herpes infection. Studies have shown that the pill form significantly reduces the number and frequency of recurrent episodes. If an episode does occur, the drug makes it shorter and less painful.

Like antibiotics, acyclovir can become less effective if used repeatedly over a long period of time. Just as scientists developed a variety of antibiotics, several antiviral drugs are now available to treat herpes. Two new drugs include valacyclovir (trade name Valtrex) and famcyclovir (trade name Famvir). In clinical studies, both have proved more effective than acyclovir in treating herpes. In a study involving 87 people experiencing their first episode of herpes, about half were treated with acyclovir and the other half with famcyclovir. Of those treated with acyclovir, 12 people reported a recurrent episode within one to six months following treatment, while only one of those treated with famcyclovir had a recurrence. Clinical studies are now being done to study how effective famyciclovir is in treating another STD—chronic hepatitis B infection. Unlike a herpes infection, a hepatitis infection can be fatal.

# 5 Hepatitis

Viral diseases are among the most widespread illnesses in humans. Some of these viral diseases are sexually transmitted. As you have just read, herpes is one such disease. Another is **hepatitis**, one of the most common serious viral diseases in the world. Like herpes, hepatitis can be transmitted through sexual contact, though the disease can also spread in other ways. Like the virus that causes herpes, the virus responsible for hepatitis comes in more than one type. In fact, scientists now know of at least six types of hepatitis viruses and each type of virus causes a different form of hepatitis. Taken together, these viruses make up an "alphabet soup" because the six known hepatitis viruses are called hepatitis A, hepatitis B, hepatitis C, hepatitis D, hepatitis E, and hepatitis G.

Of these six known viruses, the two that pose the least health threat are hepatitis A and hepatitis E. Hepatitis A is a common form of the virus, infecting over 100,000 people per year in the United States alone. This virus is usually transmitted through careless personal hygiene or by eating contaminated food, such as shellfish. Hepatitis A is a relatively mild disease that is often taken care of by the body's immune system. Hepatitis E has mainly been reported in parts of Asia, Africa, and Mexico. Like hepatitis A, this form of the disease is relatively mild and may cause nausea, fatigue, fever, loss of appetite, and a yellowish tinge to the skin. People who acquire either hepatitis A or hepatitis E develop symptoms that last anywhere from a few days to several weeks. Most of those infected with either of these hepatitis viruses do not need any special treatment other than bed rest.

The other forms of hepatitis pose a greater health threat and usually require medical attention because they do not respond as well as hepatitis A and hepatitis E to the body's immune system. Nearly 3.5 million Americans are believed to have hepatitis C, the disease that poses the greatest threat to those working in the health-care field, such as doctors, nurses, and laboratory technicians. Even hospital patients are at risk for contracting hepatitis C. For example, the legendary baseball player Mickey Mantle found out that he had this disease shortly before his death from hepatitis in 1995. Doctors

*Mickey Mantle underwent a liver transplant in his fight against hepatitis C.*

suspect that he actually became infected with the hepatitis C virus decades before when he had been operated on several times for knee surgery during his playing career. Hepatitis D can infect and cause illness only in those people already infected with hepatitis B. When the hepatitis D virus does become active in the presence of the hepatitis B virus, the combination is extremely dangerous and life-threatening. The most recently discovered form of the virus is hepatitis G, first identified in 1996. The long-term effects of this virus have yet to be discovered.

The most dangerous of all the six known types is hepatitis B. This form of hepatitis, once known as serum hepatitis, is very serious and can cause death, especially if a person becomes subsequently infected with the hepatitis D virus. Fortunately subsequent infection with hepatitis D does not occur often. Moreover, about 90 percent of adults recover from a hepatitis B infection in a few months, once their immune system has destroyed all the viruses. The remaining 10 percent of those infected with hepatitis B will either die from the disease or be affected for months, years, or even for the rest of their lives. Those who are thus affected are known as **carriers**.

A carrier is a person who continues to carry the cause of a disease for years or even for the rest of their lives. In most cases, a carrier displays no symptoms of the disease. Nonetheless, such carriers are infectious, capable of passing the disease to others. In the case of hepatitis B, a carrier is anyone who has harbored the virus in their blood for more than six months. In the United States, there are an estimated 1 million to 2 million hepatitis B carriers. This means that 1 out of every 240 people in America is a carrier. According to the United Nations World Health

Organization, some 300 million people around the world are hepatitis B carriers.

After six months, the immune system of some carriers will finally be able to rid the body of the hepatitis B virus. Most carriers, however, will continue to harbor the virus past this point in their lives. These people are said to have **chronic hepatitis**. Despite the presence of the virus, most people with chronic hepatitis experience no serious problems and lead normal healthy lives. Some do become sick, however, and may develop serious health problems, including liver cancer. Regardless of their state of health, anyone who is a hepatitis B carrier cannot donate blood while they are alive or donate organs after they die.

## The Liver

No matter what type of hepatitis virus infects the body, its target is the liver. Once inside the liver, the virus can cause extensive damage. For example, hepatitis B is the leading cause of liver cancer. Liver cancer is one of the top three causes of death in males who live in certain regions of Asia and Africa. Worldwide, approximately 25 percent of hepatitis carriers die of some form of liver disease as adults. To understand the health threat posed by hepatitis viruses, you must first know something about their target.

The liver is the body's largest internal organ, weighing about 1.5 kilograms (3 pounds). It lies just under the rib cage to the right of the stomach and spreads across the entire body. The liver is unique for several reasons. For one thing, the liver is the only internal organ that can regenerate a small portion of itself that has been either surgically removed or destroyed by disease. In addition, most organs in your body perform a single function. The heart simply pumps blood, while the lungs are solely responsible for exchanging oxygen and carbon dioxide. The liver, however, performs numerous functions in the body. In fact, the liver plays a role in just about every system in your body, including the digestive, circulatory, respiratory, and excretory systems.

All foods that are digested are absorbed by the intestines. Before these nutrients are transported to the cells, they are first brought by the bloodstream to the liver. The liver then removes and stores any nutrients that are not immediately needed by the body. For example, your body uses sugar as its primary source of energy. Every cell of your body is processing sugar to obtain the energy you need to do all that you do. If cells have enough sugar, then the liver absorbs the excess that is passing through in the bloodstream. This excess sugar is converted into a form that the liver can store. Whenever supplies run low in the body, the liver releases the stored sugar for use by the cells.

The liver also participates directly in digestion. You know from experience that oil and water do not mix. Oils are fats, one of the nutrients your body needs. Digestion can only take place in a watery environment. But how can the body digest fats in water when the two do not mix? The answer is found in the liver. The liver produces a substance called bile that breaks large fat globules into much smaller ones. These smaller fat globules can be suspended in water, allowing them to be digested by the body.

The liver also filters the blood as it passes through, removing and destroying any toxic materials that may be present. For example, the liver breaks down, or detoxifies, drugs and alcohol that have been absorbed by the blood and turns them into harmless substances that are eliminated by the body. In effect, the liver is the "detox center" of the body. Another toxic material that the liver gets rid of is ammonia, which is so highly poisonous that it cannot remain for long in the body. Ammonia is produced by the body as part of its digestive process. The liver combines ammonia with carbon dioxide produced in respiration to form a nontoxic substance that is eliminated in the urine. Others jobs involving the liver include blood clotting and the control of cholesterol levels in the body. It's no wonder that any disease, such as hepatitis, that affects the liver is considered very serious.

## Hepatitis B

Of all the forms of hepatitis, hepatitis B is the only one that qualifies as a true STD. Hepatitis A and E are mainly transmitted by consuming food or water contaminated with the virus. Hepatitis C is mainly a risk to those who receive a blood transfusion or inject drugs into their body. Hepatitis G was thought to be transmitted only through infected blood, but recent evidence indicates that it may also be sexually transmitted. More studies will have to be done before scientists know for sure. Recall that hepatitis D infects those already infected with hepatitis B. So that leaves hepatitis B.

Each year, some 300,000 people in the United States get hepatitis B, mainly as a result of heterosexual intercourse. Between 10 million and 30 million people become infected each year worldwide. If the infection is not cured, the hepatitis B virus destroys liver cells. Recall that the liver can replace cells that are either removed or destroyed. However, the liver cannot regenerate if too many of its cells are affected. Thus chronic or long-term infection may destroy the liver, leading to a condition known as **cirrhosis**. Between 4,000 and 5,000 people die each year in the United States from cirrhosis caused by the hepatitis B virus. Worldwide, hepatitis B infection leads to more than 1 million deaths every year.

About half the people who are infected by the hepatitis B virus never develop any symptoms. The other half of those who are infected develop symptoms about four weeks after infection, but the incubation period can last anywhere from two to seven weeks. Symptoms of a hepatitis infection include pains in the muscles, joints, or stomach, vomiting or diarrhea, loss of appetite, fatigue, and a yellowish color in the skin or eyes. A yellowish color in the skin or eyes is a condition known as **jaundice**. Jaundice is a clear indication that a person has been infected with a hepatitis virus. As liver cells are destroyed by the virus, a substance normally destroyed by the liver begins to accumulate in the blood. This substance gives the blood and, in turn, the skin and eyes, a yellowish color. Those who develop jaundice also usually produce a dark urine and have itching of the skin.

## Transmission

You have learned that half the people infected with hepatitis B never develop symptoms, and those who do are infectious even before symptoms appear. Thus the virus has a good chance of being transmitted without anyone being aware of what is happening. In fact, an estimated 40 percent of people who have been infected with hepatitis B have no idea how or when they became infected.

The virus can pass through a tiny break in the skin. Once inside the body, the virus can thrive in the blood or **semen**, the fluid a male produces that contains sperm. Because the virus is carried in body fluids, it can be transmitted by an infected person who engages in either vaginal, oral, or anal sex. The virus can also be transmitted from an infected pregnant woman to her newborn baby during delivery.

The virus can also be transmitted in a number of other ways. It can even enter a tiny break in the skin. It can be transmitted by sharing a toothbrush or razor with someone who is infected. In this case, the toothbrush or razor must first be exposed to the blood or another body fluid of the infected person. The hepatitis virus can also be transmitted with a contaminated needle used to make a tattoo. However, the virus cannot be transmitted by shaking hands, sharing food, hugging, or visiting an infected person. These forms of casual contact are not likely to result in the passing of body fluids between people.

Because of the numerous ways hepatitis B can be transmitted and because of the serious nature of the disease, the Occupational Safety and Health Administration of the federal government issued a list of people it considered to be at high risk of contracting hepatitis B. This list, issued in 1992, includes people who work in medical offices, dental offices, hospitals, drug-treatment centers, and nursing homes; people who repair medical and dental equipment; people who are involved in blood collection and processing; and people in the funeral business. Despite the warnings and precautions taken, approximately two health-care workers are infected each day with the hepatitis B virus.

# Treatment

Anyone who has reason to think that they may have been infected with the hepatitis B virus should see a doctor for a blood test, which is the only way the disease can be diagnosed. Many people learn that they have hepatitis B when they donate blood, which is routinely tested for the virus. The blood test, however, may not reveal that a person has been infected until two to six months after the virus has invaded the body.

About 90 percent of adults recover from hepatitis B within a few months, the time it takes for their immune system to destroy the virus. These people have developed an immunity to the disease and will never get it again. However, blood tests will always show that they have been infected with the hepatitis B virus. As a result, blood centers will not accept their blood.

For the 10 percent of adults whose immune systems do not wipe out the virus, treatment should begin immediately. People infected with hepatitis B need to get plenty of rest, drink lots of fluids, and limit the amount of fat in their diet. Reducing one's intake of fats puts less strain on the liver, where fats are stored until they are needed by the body. Another way to put less strain on the liver is to avoid alcohol and certain medications that have been prescribed by their doctors. As the body's "detox center," part of the liver's job is to take any excess medication and convert it into harmless substances. Thus the infected person may be told by a doctor to avoid taking certain prescribed medications until the treatment for hepatitis is finished.

The current recommended treatment for hepatitis B is interferon. **Interferons** are proteins that the body produces in response to a viral infection.

Scientists have developed ways to mass-produce these interferons for use against certain diseases, including hepatitis B. Unfortunately, interferon treatment produces a number of undesirable side effects including chills, fever, headaches, fatigue, and loss of appetite. These effects can last for the first few weeks of treatment. But if the patient can bear the side effects, the outlook is promising. Studies have shown that interferon is quite effective in treating hepatitis B. In one case, 65 percent of those receiving interferon were free of the virus five years after their treatment.

A doctor may also prescribe an antiviral drug to treat the hepatitis infection. One such drug is lamivudine, and other antiviral drugs are also being tested. So far the results have been promising. In a study involving more than 2,000 carriers infected with hepatitis B, the antiviral drug being tested proved to be most effective in preventing serious liver damage. Doctors are also testing combinations of antiviral drugs to reduce the chances of promoting the development of viruses that will become resistant to treatment.

## Prevention

Chapter 9 describes the various preventive measures a person can take to avoid getting an STD. But one important step that can be taken to prevent getting hepatitis B is not available for any other STD—**vaccination**. Vaccination is the procedure in which a harmless version of a pathogen is introduced into the body. In response, the body produces antibodies and develops an immunity to the disease. As an infant, you received vaccinations against several diseases, including mumps, polio, and measles. Should the pathogens that cause these diseases invade your body, your immune system will immediately recognize them and destroy them before they have had a chance to cause any damage. In some cases, the protection offered by a vaccination wears off over time. That's why doctors recommend that people get periodic "booster" shots to restore their immunity against certain diseases, such as polio and tetanus.

The history of vaccinations started in 1796 when a British doctor named Edward Jenner saw a connection between a deadly disease in humans— smallpox—and a related but harmless disease in cows called cowpox. Jenner knew that dairymaids who milked the cows were immune to smallpox, a disease that left disfiguring marks on the body including the face. Jenner reasoned that if a person were vaccinated with cowpox, an immunity against smallpox should also develop. Jenner finally had the chance to test his theory when a dairymaid contracted cowpox. He took a sample from a sore on the

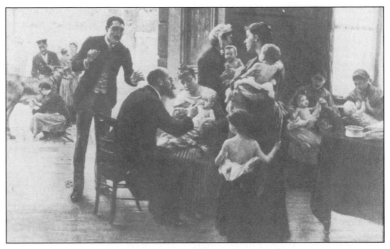

*Edward Jenner is shown inoculating patients with the smallpox vaccine.*

woman's hand and injected it into an eight-year-old boy. Two months later, Jenner injected the boy with a sample taken from the sore on a person with smallpox. The boy never developed smallpox even though Jenner injected him with smallpox material several times. Jenner called his procedure *vaccination*, after *vacca*, the Latin word for cow.

About 200 years later, scientists developed a vaccination against hepatitis B. The vaccination is recommended for anyone who is in close contact with an infected person. These include people who have a close relative infected with hepatitis B, those who work with blood, and anyone who is listed by the Occupational Safety and Health Administration as being at risk of contracting the disease. In addition, babies born to mothers with hepatitis B should also be vaccinated. This would greatly reduce their chances of becoming a hepatitis carrier later in life. The vaccination consists of a series of three injections that are administered into a muscle of the thigh or upper arm. No booster shots are required, and it is never too late to start.

As with any vaccination, there is an extremely small risk that serious problems, or even death, could occur. But the chances of developing serious or even fatal problems by getting hepatitis B are much greater. And the vaccine against hepatitis B is one of the safest vaccines. Doctors highly recommend that those at risk, and even all babies, get vaccinated. A vaccinated person may experience some minor side effects such as a redness or soreness that develops in the injected area. The person may also develop a mild to moderate fever. If this happens, an aspirin-free pain reliever can be taken until the side effects disappear. Studies have shown that the vaccination is highly effective, preventing the disease in 95 percent of those who are at high risk of getting hepatitis B. Unfortunately, those who are already infected with the hepatitis B virus will not benefit from the vaccination.

The vaccination against hepatitis was first used in 1982. Since that time, hundreds of millions of people have been vaccinated against hepatitis B. In 1992, the United Nations recommended that all countries include the vaccine as part of their regular immunization program. Why did it take 10 years before the United Nations recommended that the vaccine should be used on a worldwide basis? One reason was a concern that the vaccine could transmit another disease that is far deadlier than hepatitis— AIDS. Concerns about the hepatitis vaccine transmitting AIDS, however, were unfounded. The procedure used to prepare the hepatitis vaccine makes it impossible for the pathogen that causes AIDS to survive. But the pathogen responsible for AIDS has resisted a lot of other attempts to deal with it, as you will see in the next two chapters.

# 6 HIV

The STD that frightens people most is **AIDS**, which stands for **acquired immune deficiency syndrome**. The reason for this fear is justified. Any individual who develops AIDS will die of the disease. Despite all the best efforts of scientists throughout the world, there is still no cure for AIDS. Scientists, however, have developed various treatments that can prolong the life of a person with AIDS. But before discussing AIDS, let's take a close look at the virus that causes this disease—the **human immunodeficiency virus**, known simply as **HIV**. HIV is an interesting virus for several reasons. To understand what makes it unusual, let's first examine what viruses in general can do after they have infected a cell.

As you learned in Chapter 1, a virus is not considered a living thing. It cannot reproduce and in fact, it cannot carry out any life process on its own. A virus does not need food, water, oxygen, or anything that living things must have to survive. A virus needs only two things—the right temperature, and freedom from toxic chemicals and the body's immune system. If these two conditions are met, a virus can remain intact and untouched forever. But if the temperature is too hot or too cold, or if the virus is exposed to toxic chemicals or the body's immune system, the virus will likely be destroyed. In the meantime, the virus can just remain as it is, unless it is destroyed or infects a host cell.

Once it infects a host cell, the virus can take charge and direct the production of new viruses, using the cell's "machinery" to do so. The production of new viruses inside a host cell is called **viral replication**. Chapter 1 explained that a virus consists of a protein coat surrounding a nucleic acid—either DNA or RNA. Both DNA and RNA viruses must first attach themselves to a host cell. To help them attach, the viruses use projections extending from their protein coat to bind themselves to the host cell. Once attached, one of the viruses begins to inject its nucleic acid into the host cell. After its nucleic acid has been injected into the host cell, viruses differ in the way they use the cell's "machinery" to replicate. What happens next depends on whether the virus contains DNA or RNA.

A DNA virus may immediately start taking over the host cell's "machinery" to produce new viruses. This is called the **lytic cycle** of a virus, and it consists of five steps. The first step is the attachment of the virus to the host cell. The host cell must have a specific site that the virus can recognize. If not, the virus cannot attach itself and infect the cell. For example, the hepatitis virus can attach and infect only liver cells because these cells are the only ones with a site that the virus can recognize. The herpes virus can attach and infect only skin cells for the same reason.

In the second step, the virus releases a chemical that bores open a hole in the host cell. The third step involves injection of the DNA into the host cell. During the fourth step, the viral DNA takes control of the cell's "machinery" and begins the process of replication. A single virus can produce about 100 new viruses in only 20 minutes. In the fifth and final step, the virus causes the host cell to make a chemical that breaks open the cell, releasing the newly formed viruses to infect other cells. Obviously, this step results in the death of the host cell.

A DNA virus may also enter a **lysogenic cycle**, in which the virus infects a host cell without causing its immediate destruction. During a lysogenic cycle, the DNA that the virus has injected becomes incorporated into the DNA of the host cell. Here the viral DNA does no harm; it does everything that the host cell's DNA does. A virus may remain in a lysogenic cycle for days, months, or even years. When the herpes virus retreats to hide in nerve cells, it enters its lysogenic cycle where it can remain for a long period of time. Once activated, however, the virus can emerge from its lysogenic cycle and enter its lytic cycle where it begins both its own replication and the host cell's destruction.

RNA viruses behave somewhat differently from DNA viruses. Some RNA viruses, known as **retroviruses**, contain a special enzyme. An **enzyme** is a chemical that can speed up the rate of a chemical reaction. The enzyme that retroviruses contain is called **reverse transcriptase**. This name is derived from the fact that this enzyme reverses the course of what usually happens in a cell. Normally, DNA directs the making of RNA. But when reverse transcriptase is present, RNA can direct the making of DNA. Thus, the RNA that the virus injects into a host cell can direct the making of viral DNA. This viral DNA can then enter either a lysogenic cycle by joining with the host cell DNA or enter a lytic cycle and begin viral replication.

# HIV

HIV is the most complex and thoroughly studied virus in scientific history. HIV is a retrovirus. Two groups of retroviruses that can infect humans are known. One group includes oncoretroviruses. The prefix *onco-* refers to cancer. Obviously, oncoretroviruses are responsible for certain types of cancer in humans, including some forms of leukemia. The second group of retroviruses consist of lentiviruses. HIV is a lentivirus. The prefix *lenti-* means slow. Obviously, lentiviruses do their damage slowly, sometimes very slowly as in the case of HIV and AIDS.

Five types or strains of HIV have been identified —HIV strains A, B, C, D, and E. Each HIV strain has a slightly different genetic makeup. For reasons that are not known, certain strains are more prevalent in certain parts of the world. For example HIV strain B is the major type found in both North and South America, while HIV strain E is limited to certain areas in Asia. Three of the strains —A, C, and D—are found in Africa. No matter what strain the virus is, HIV is roughly spherical in shape. The outer coat consists of proteins that are combined with sugars. Inside this coat are two copies of the viral RNA, along with four viral proteins and three enzymes. One of these enzymes is the reverse transcriptase that HIV will need to begin replication inside its host cell. The other two enzymes are also needed by HIV to finish the process.

One of the unusual aspects of HIV is its ability to infect not just one cell type, but several different cell types. All these cell types have something in common though—they are white blood cells and part of the immune system. Because of the nature of its targets, HIV is most effective in destroying the body's main defense against invading pathogens. As you will see in the next chapter, this destruction leads to all sorts of problems. The two main targets of HIV are specialized white blood cells called **CD4 T-lymphocytes** and **macrophages**. Both of these cells are crucial if the immune system is to function properly. These two types of white blood cells have a chemical compound on their surface that a protein on the coat of HIV readily recognizes. So attachment to its target cell, the first step in a viral infection, is an easy task for HIV once it has invaded the body.

After it has attached to a white blood cell, HIV begins the next step. A protein on the HIV coat combines or fuses with the surface of the host cell. This fusion opens a hole through which the virus can inject its RNA into the host cell. In fact, HIV injects all its core materials—its two RNA copies, its four proteins, and its three enzymes—into the host cell. The reverse transcriptase immediately begins directing the viral RNA to make viral DNA. What follows next is quite complicated. Simply put, the injected materials turn the viral DNA into a form that can become part of the host cell DNA. In effect, all that remains of the HIV is a piece of viral DNA that is integrated into the host cell DNA. HIV has entered its lysogenic cycle.

While in its lysogenic cycle, the viral DNA allows the cell to continue all its normal routines, including the process of producing new white blood cells. In this process, called **mitosis**, a cell divides to produce two new cells. Before a cell can undergo mitosis, it must first make a complete copy of all its DNA. As you read in Chapter 1, nucleic acids are the carriers of hereditary information. DNA is the nucleic acid that contains the genetic "blueprints." RNA is the nucleic acid that helps translate these "blueprints" into reality, just as a builder "translates" an architect's blueprints into a house. After the cell's DNA has been copied, each of the two cells produced in mitosis receives a complete set of the genetic "blueprints."

But now the DNA of a white blood cell infected with HIV contains the virus's DNA. So each time the cell makes a copy of its own DNA, it also makes a copy of the virus's DNA. Also, each time it passes its own DNA onto the new cells it produces in mitosis, it passes on a copy of the virus's DNA. HIV continues to spread in the body every time one of its target cells divides. Because the virus remains in its lysogenic cycle, however, no notice is taken of this spreading danger.

## HIV's Genetic "Blueprints"

You learned that one interesting aspect of HIV is its ability to infect several different types of cells. Another interesting aspect is the nature of HIV's genetic "blueprints." Its genetic information is extremely simple. Genetic information is bundled in packets called genes. A **gene** is the functional unit of heredity. Genes normally make up the DNA, the hereditary material in all living things. In HIV, however, genes make up the RNA, which is the hereditary material of retroviruses. The RNA of HIV consists of three major genes and six smaller ones, for a total of nine genes. Contrast this to the situation in humans. Scientists estimate that the DNA in one human cell contains 50,000 genes!

The three major genes in HIV are called *gag, env,* and *pol.* The *gag* gene is responsible for making the four proteins found inside the viral coat. The *env* gene directs the production of the proteins that form the viral coat. The *pol* gene is responsible for making the three enzymes that are packaged inside the coat, including reverse transcriptase. Together, these three genes make up more than 70 percent of the RNA in the virus. The other six genes that make up the remaining 30 percent of the RNA play various roles in the infection cycle of HIV. In contrast to the genes of HIV, scientists are just beginning to unlock the various roles of the thousands of genes in human DNA.

Despite its simple nature, the RNA of HIV is quite deceiving. The deception is caused by the reverse transcriptase enzyme. Recall that reverse transcriptase makes it possible for RNA to direct the production of DNA. Both RNA and DNA are made from small building blocks called **nucleotides**. Each nucleic acid contains four different nucleotides. In the case of DNA, these four nucleotides are abbreviated A, T, G, and C. In the case of RNA, the four nucleotides are abbreviated A, U, G, and C. Notice that DNA and RNA share three nucleotides—A, G, and C. They differ in only one nucleotide. DNA contains T, while RNA contains U.

Nucleotides often come in pairs—A with T (or A with U in the case of RNA) and G with C. Thus if an RNA consists of the sequence A-G-C-C-U-A-G-U-U, then reverse transcriptase would produce a DNA with the sequence T-C-G-G-A-T-C-A-A. However, the reverse transcriptase in HIV makes frequent errors so that the wrong nucleotide is inserted into the DNA that the viral RNA makes when it infects a host cell. This creates all kinds of problems for the body's immune system. To understand why, you must first look at how the body's immune system normally reacts to a viral invader.

## The Immune Response

Whenever a pathogen invades the body, white blood cells launch an attack known as the **immune response**. To launch an effective attack that can destroy the pathogen, the cells must be able to distinguish between a foreign invader and the body's own cells. To do this, white blood cells known as **lymphocytes** have proteins scattered over their surface. A lymphocyte is a white blood cell that makes up the body's specific defense against pathogens. The proteins on the surface of a lymphocyte have a distinct three-dimensional shape. These proteins are called **receptors**. The immune system makes millions of different kinds of lymphocytes, each with uniquely shaped receptors on its surface. You read earlier that a virus recognizes a specific site on its target cell, which might be a lymphocyte. The reverse is also true. A receptor on a lymphocyte may recognize a specific site on a virus.

A foreign invader, such as a virus, carries various chemical substances on its surface, including proteins. One of these substances may have a shape that fits with that of the receptor on a lymphocyte. If the two shapes fit, then the pathogen and lymphocyte will bind. If not, the pathogen will escape detection—at least for the moment. Consider what happens when a cold virus invades the body. The pathogen eventually enters the bloodstream where it encounters a lymphocyte. The receptors on the first lymphocyte that the cold virus encounters may not match anything on the virus's surface. So the cold virus escapes detection by the lymphocyte.

However, the cold virus will eventually come across a lymphocyte with receptors that match. When this happens, the lymphocyte will mount an immune response. Anything that brings about an immune response is called an **antigen**.

The immune response involves an attack on the invader that includes the production of antibodies, which you read about in Chapter 3. The attack actually starts, however, with macrophages. Like a lymphocyte, a macrophage has receptors that can bind to the antigens on a pathogen and initiate the immune response. The macrophage first "swallows up" and destroys the pathogen. Then the macrophage displays fragments of the pathogen's antigens on its own surface. Earlier you read that a macrophage is one of the cells that HIV infects and destroys. Obviously, if HIV destroys macrophages, then the immune response will be affected. If enough macrophages are destroyed by HIV, then the immune response may not be activated at all. In this case, the body is wide open to an attack by any pathogen that can successfully invade the body. As you will see in the next chapter, a number of pathogens are capable of doing this.

Recall that HIV can also infect and destroy lymphocytes, specifically CD4 T-lymphocytes. You read earlier that lymphocytes have receptors that can bind to a pathogen and destroy it. Thus both macrophages and lymphocytes can mount an immune response only when their receptors can bind to the pathogen. Here's where HIV proves elusive. Recall that the reverse transcriptase enzyme in HIV makes frequent errors when the virus's RNA is making DNA. For example, the RNA sequence G-U-C-C-A-G-G-U-A may mistakenly make the DNA sequence C-A-G-G-T-G-C-A-T. What is the correct sequence that the RNA should make? What happens after the mistake is made is rather complicated. All you need to realize is that this mistake results in HIV making a different protein during the lytic cycle. This protein will be assembled into the new coat the virus is making inside the host cell.

The reverse transcriptase in HIV makes mistakes all the time. Thus new proteins are constantly being assembled into the virus's coat. This creates havoc for both macrophages and lymphocytes. You read in Chapter 2 that the immune system normally develops a "memory." If a white blood cell sees the same pathogen again, the immune system can respond faster and in greater force. But if HIV is constantly changing its surface proteins, the white blood cells are always facing a "new" invader and never have a chance to develop a "memory." As a result, HIV can infect and destroy the white blood cells before they have the chance to destroy the virus.

This constant changing of surface proteins poses another problem. You read in Chapter 5 that scientists have developed a vaccination against hepatitis B. This vaccine is made by injecting a small amount of a weakened or dead form of the pathogen into a person. This process is done several times to promote the development of a "memory" by the person's immune system. Should the actual pathogen, such as the hepatitis B virus, invade the body, then the immune system will be ready. However, all attempts to develop a vaccine against HIV have failed because of the constantly changing nature of the virus's protein coat. As long as HIV continues to change its protein coat, vaccination against HIV seems unlikely.

# Transmission

Now that you know how HIV infects and destroys cells, you should next examine how the virus is transmitted. Obviously, sexual contact—either vaginal, oral, or anal—is the primary method by which HIV is transmitted. Because HIV is carried in the blood, the virus can actually be transmitted anytime this body fluid is exchanged between two people. Other modes of transmission include the sharing of contaminated needles or transfusion of infected blood. To prevent transmission by transfusion, all donated blood is routinely screened for HIV. Of course, blood will not be accepted for donation from anyone who is already infected with the virus.

Unfortunately, routine screening of blood samples was not performed until many people had been infected with HIV by receiving a transfusion of blood

*Sexually active teens could be at risk for transmission of HIV as well as other STDs.*

that was contaminated. This method of transmission occurred frequently in people, especially children, with hemophilia. Hemophilia is a disease in which the person's blood cannot clot. People who have this disease need frequent transfusions, either of whole blood or the purified factors that are involved in clotting. Routine screening of all donated blood samples has now eliminated this danger.

Transmission of HIV can also occur between a mother and her newborn baby. This may happen before birth, during delivery, or even after birth if the mother breast-feeds the baby. Health-care workers are especially warned about the risk of transmission. Such workers usually become infected by accidentally sticking themselves with contaminated needles. In several cases, health-care workers have become infected with HIV after contaminated blood has come in contact with an open cut or has splashed into their eyes or inside their nose. So far, only one case has been documented in which an infected dentist transmitted the virus to six patients. A study of more than 22,000 patients of 63 HIV-infected doctors and dentists has not revealed another case of this type of transmission.

HIV has also been transmitted between family members living together in the same household. This mode of transmission, which is very rare, is believed to occur when a family member comes in direct contact with infected blood. Precautions that can be taken include the wearing of gloves to prevent any direct contact with blood or other body fluids that might contain blood such as urine or vomit. Any cut, sore, or break in the skin of a family member who is infected with HIV should be properly bandaged.

Fortunately, HIV does not survive outside the human body. Studies have shown that the virus can be kept alive for days or weeks in the laboratory only under very limited and controlled conditions. Once these conditions are no longer present, the virus loses its ability to infect cells within several hours. Because it cannot survive well outside the body, transmission of HIV through air, water, food, or other animals is very unlikely. Concerns have been raised about the possibility of transmission by biting and bloodsucking insects, such as mosquitoes. Studies have shown no evidence of transmission through insects, even in regions of the world such as Africa where both HIV and mosquitoes are widespread. When a mosquito bites a person, it injects its saliva, not its blood. The saliva may contain the pathogen that causes malaria, but it does not contain HIV, which cannot survive and reproduce in insects.

HIV has been found in the saliva and tears of people infected with HIV. However, the quantity of the virus present in such samples has been so low that scientists suspect it could not be effectively transmitted to another person. On the other hand, HIV has never been isolated from the sweat of HIV-infected people. In any case, contact with the saliva, tears, or sweat of a person infected with HIV has never been found to result in the transmission of the virus.

The ways in which HIV can be transmitted have been clearly identified. Once infected with HIV, a person is certain to develop AIDS at some point in the future. Recall that there is no cure for AIDS and no vaccination against HIV. Thus, the only recourse is not to become infected with the virus. Again, specific steps to take to avoid infection by HIV and subsequent development of AIDS are described in Chapter 9.

# 7 AIDS

Throughout history, epidemics have come and gone. An **epidemic** is a contagious disease capable of spreading rapidly through human populations. Usually epidemics develop quickly, cause widespread illness or death, and then mysteriously disappear, often just as quickly as they came. An epidemic may or may not be deadly. In the past—before the advent of antibiotics—most epidemics killed many people. You read in Chapter 3 about the syphilis epidemic that swept across Europe during the late 1400s and early 1500s, killing an estimated 10 million people. This, however, was not the first recorded epidemic. Around 430 B.C., a Greek historian wrote about a devastating disease that wiped out most of the population of Athens. Other epidemics would follow. During the second and third centuries A.D., historians believe that epidemics of smallpox and measles raged through the Mediterranean area.

In middle of the sixth century, a deadly epidemic suddenly appeared and spread throughout Europe. The epidemic involved a disease known as bubonic plague, a highly contagious and usually fatal disease. Nearly 90 percent of those who became infected died of the disease in less than a week. Millions of people died of bubonic plague. After causing its death and destruction, the plague would quickly vanish. This cycle of appearing and disappearing continued into the eighth century. For some 500 years after that, Europe was happily free of the plague. But then in the middle of the 1300s, it suddenly appeared again, this time more deadly than ever. Epidemics of bubonic plague took a total of more than 135 million lives in Europe.

Between 1918 and 1919, just as World War I was ending, another epidemic erupted. This was an outbreak of a fatal strain of a disease called influenza. Caused by a virus, influenza primarily affects the respiratory system. The impact of the influenza epidemic was even greater than that of earlier epidemics. While the bubonic plague was limited to Europe, influenza spread all over the world. People living in close quarters were especially susceptible to influenza. Because people throughout the world were affected by influenza, this disease was a **pandemic**. A pandemic is an epidemic that is not confined to a

*The medical community took extra precautions before making hospital rounds during the influenza pandemic of 1918-19.*

single continent such as Europe or North America but affects people all over the world.

The influenza pandemic started in the United States in March 1918, claiming its first victim at a military camp in Kansas. Within seven days, every state in the country had been infected. In a month, the virus had spread to China and Japan. The next month, influenza claimed lives in Africa and South America. When it was all over, the influenza pandemic had caused between 25 million and 35 million deaths throughout the world in only 18 months. The disease then suddenly disappeared. Fortunately, it has never shown up again. But a new pandemic has recently appeared and today threatens lives all over the world—AIDS.

## History of AIDS

The first medical report of a living person having AIDS was recorded in 1981. At that time, Michael Gottlieb, a research scientist at the University of California in Los Angeles, was interested in the workings of the immune system. He began looking in local hospitals for patients with an immune deficiency disease, which develops only when a person's immune system is not functioning properly. The first such patient Gottlieb discovered was a young man who was suffering from a yeast infection that had spread to his throat. The young man also had a rare pneumonia that would not respond to treatment with antibiotics. Gottlieb decided to try out a new technique for counting T-lymphocytes, known simply as T-cells, to help this young man.

In Chapter 6, you learned that HIV infects T-cells, which play a crucial role in the immune system. The young man turned out to have a very low T-cell count. Gottlieb felt he was on the right track, believing that the young man's pneumonia was an immune deficiency disease. Gottlieb decided to search for more patients with a similar condition.

Gottlieb discovered three more such patients in the next few months. Each was a young man who had a yeast infection in his throat and an active case of pneumonia. All the men had low T-cell counts. Gottlieb called the local health department to report his findings and inquire if they knew of any similar cases. One of the people working at the health department found one other case, bringing the total in the Los Angeles area to five. Gottlieb also became aware of one more fact—all the men were homosexuals.

While Gottlieb was working in Los Angeles, researchers on the other side of the United States were making an interesting observation. Working at various New York City hospitals, researchers dis-

*Dr. Michael Gottlieb, who pioneered AIDS research in the early 1980s, makes an address at a press conference in 1985.*

covered groups of homosexual men who had a rare form of cancer known as Kaposi's sarcoma. This disease develops when the immune system is deficient and shows up as purple blotches on the skin. All these findings, including those made by Gottlieb, were reported to the Centers for Disease Control (CDC) in Atlanta, Georgia. The CDC monitors disease patterns and looks for possible epidemics.

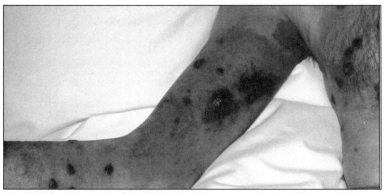

*Dark blotches or skin lesions characteristic of Kaposi's sarcoma cover the body of a man suffering from AIDS.*

Studying the reports coming in from Los Angeles and New York, staff members at the CDC believed they were looking at the first signs of a newly emerging and potentially epidemic disease that involved the immune system. The disease seemed to be transmitted among young homosexual men. On June 5, 1981, the CDC made its first official announcement about the mysterious disease. The report contained information about the five patients in the Los Angeles area, pointing out three characteristics they shared: the patients were men in their twenties, they were homosexual, and they had an unusual type of pneumonia. At first, the CDC called the disease "gay cancer" but soon renamed it GRID (Gay-Related Immune Deficiency). In 1981, 128 homosexual men died in the United States of this disease. In 1982, the disease became known as AIDS (Acquired Immune Deficiency Syndrome). This disease seemed to be killing everyone who developed it, and the number of those afflicted was growing rapidly. In 1982, 460 homosexual men in the United States died of AIDS, nearly four times the number of deaths caused by the disease in the previous year.

Although it was first recognized officially in 1981 and received its current name in 1982, AIDS probably has a slightly older history. But compared to other STDs, AIDS is still a relative newcomer, apparently making its first appearance in the early 1970s. At that time, people were dying from a previously unreported epidemic disease. This disease was difficult to transmit, remained "quiet" for a long period of time, and then proved fatal. This disease may have been AIDS. More substantial evidence would be provided by a blood test that was developed in 1984 to detect HIV infection and approved for use a year later. Frozen blood samples taken from people who had died of hepatitis B during the 1970s were tested for HIV infection. Some of the test results were positive. Test results performed on pre-1970 blood samples were negative, supporting the belief that AIDS had first appeared in the early 1970s, but had gone undetected.

The blood samples that were tested had been taken from people who had lived in other countries, allowing scientists to pinpoint where AIDS first appeared on the world scene. In the United States and Sweden, the disease first appeared exclusively among homosexual men. In other parts of the world such as Haiti and Tanzania, AIDS had infected both males and females. By appearing in areas all over the world, AIDS qualified as a pandemic. Today we know that AIDS is a disease that can affect anyone, regardless of sexual preference, age, nationality, race, or social status.

*Demonstrations such as this one outside the United Nations are aimed at increasing public awareness and support in the fight against AIDS.*

# Diagnosing HIV

As you know, a blood test was developed in 1984 that can determine if a person has been infected with HIV. The test works by detecting the antibodies the body makes after being infected by HIV, rather than the virus itself. Since 1984, a second test for HIV has been developed. This test also detects the antibodies the body makes, rather than detecting HIV directly. Both tests are often used to determine if a person is infected with HIV. Results from this two-part testing are more than 99 percent accurate.

Following HIV infection, the body takes several weeks to produce the antibodies that both tests look for. Thus, someone who has been infected with the virus within the last 12 weeks has probably not produced enough antibodies yet for either test to detect. In that case, the test result may be a false negative—the person is infected with HIV, but the test fails to reveal it. Anyone who has reason to suspect HIV infection should be retested after enough time has passed for the body to produce antibodies, usually three to six weeks.

The first test developed for HIV is called the **enzyme linked immunoabsorbent assay (ELISA or EIA)**. In this test, a blood sample is incubated with proteins that are unique to HIV. If antibodies against HIV are present in the blood, they will react with these proteins and the solution in which they are incubated will change color, giving a positive result. The second test for HIV is called the **western blot**. The HIV proteins are placed as distinct spots on a strip of special paper. A blood sample is applied to these spots. If antibodies are present, the color will change, producing dark bands on the paper strip. A certain combination of these bands will

97

indicate a positive result. Usually, a blood sample is first tested with ELISA. If positive, the test is repeated. If still positive, the Western blot test is used. If this test result is also positive, then the person is diagnosed as being infected with HIV.

Two additional tests for HIV infection have recently become available for use at home. One test is known as a "home sampling kit." With this kit, a person takes his or her own blood sample at home by pricking a finger, blotting it on a special piece of paper, and then sending it off to a laboratory for testing. A few days later, the person calls up a special number, gives their personal identification code number from the kit, and is given the test result over the phone. If the result is positive, the person is offered counseling and advice as to what to do next. Another test is the "home testing kit." With this kit, a person can perform the entire test procedure at home. The advantages to this kit are the convenience, privacy,

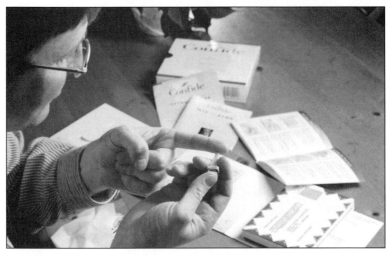

*An AIDS home-testing kit allows a person to check his or her own blood for HIV infection in the privacy of home.*

and anonymity that it offers. The disadvantage is the lack of quality control. Having a trained professional perform the test in a laboratory setting is more reliable than having a person do it at home. In addition, obtaining a positive HIV result is usually a very upsetting experience. Doing the test completely at home can place a person in the situation of not having someone available for immediate counseling or advice.

## Diagnosing AIDS

Being positive for HIV does not mean that a person has AIDS. The average time between becoming infected with HIV and developing AIDS is 8 to 10 years. Some people develop AIDS sooner, though, while others have been infected with HIV for 15 years or more with no signs of having AIDS. Exactly why some people develop AIDS faster than others is one of the many mysteries that scientists are currently trying to solve. But apparently HIV can remain in its lysogenic cycle for a long time before emerging to cause the destruction that characterizes AIDS.

To be diagnosed as having AIDS, a person must not only test positive for HIV but must also have one of the "AIDS indicator illnesses." The most common such illness is pneumocystis carinii pneumonia, abbreviated PCP. PCP is an infection that clogs the lungs, making it difficult to breathe. PCP is cause by a bacterium that many people have in their bodies. This bacterium is normally harmless, but people with a weakened immune system due to an HIV infection are not able to keep this bacterium in check. The bacterium multiplies, leading to PCP. The disease can be treated by taking an antibiotic on a regular basis.

In addition to being HIV-positive and having an AIDS indicator illness, the CDC has determined that an adolescent or adult who is diagnosed with AIDS must have a CD4 T-lymphocyte cell count, or **CD4 count**, of less than 200 cells per cubic millimeter of blood. As you know, these T-cells, known simply as T4 cells, are one of the cell types that HIV infects. In its lytic cycle, HIV destroys T4 cells, significantly reducing the number of T4 cells that circulate in the blood. Normally, T4 cells make up more than 25 percent of all the T-cells in the blood. A healthy person will have a CD4 count of at least 500, while a person diagnosed with AIDS will have 200.

## Opportunistic Infections

With a low CD4 count, a person with AIDS is susceptible to developing a number of other infections. Such infections are referred to as **opportunistic infections**. These infections are caused by microorganisms that normally pose no danger to the body. However, because their immune system is depressed, people with AIDS "provide an opportunity" for these microorganisms to cause disease and eventually death. You have already read about three such diseases—the pneumonia and throat infection Gottlieb discovered in five hospital patients in Los Angeles and the Kaposi's sarcoma seen in homosexual men in New York City. These diseases rarely appear in people who do not have AIDS.

Another opportunistic infection is caused by a herpes virus known as the **cytomegalovirus (CMV)**. This virus is related to the herpes simplex viruses discussed in Chapter 4. Many people are infected with CMV all their lives with little or no ill effects. In people with AIDS, however, the virus can cause extensive damage. Perhaps the most serious is a severe inflammation of the **retina** in the eye. The retina is the light-sensitive layer of the eye. It receives light signals that are sent to the brain where they are then interpreted as images. Inflammation of the retina can result in serious bleeding or cause the retina to become detached from the rest of the eye. In either case, blindness may result.

Sometimes people with AIDS develop **anemia**, a condition in which the blood does not have enough oxygen. Cells need oxygen to produce the energy that the body needs. Without sufficient oxygen, cells cannot supply enough energy, and the person feels tired most of the time. In this case, the anemia is usually caused by a virus that is not harmful to healthy people. But in people with AIDS and a depressed immune system, the virus prevents the body from making enough red blood cells. These are the cells that transport oxygen in the blood. The fewer the number of red blood cells, the less oxygen is transported, and the less energy is produced by the cells of the body.

Other opportunistic infections in people with AIDS are caused by yeast. As you read in Chapter 1, yeast are single-celled organisms that grow in colonies. People with AIDS can develop various yeast infections, each one caused by a different type of yeast. One type causes the throat infection that Gottlieb noticed. A different yeast type causes a serious lung disease. Another type is responsible for a painful condition that gives the mouth a white, patchy appearance. Still another type of yeast can infect the brain and spinal cord, leading to an inflammation known as **meningitis**.

Opportunistic infections may also be caused by **protists**. Protists are single-celled organisms that are more complex than bacteria, as you learned in Chapter 1. People with AIDS may develop high fevers and diarrhea that are a result of a protist infection. Once again, healthy people may be infected by the same protist without experiencing any damage. However, in people with AIDS, the protist can produce an infection that may lead to destruction of brain tissue.

Treatment for almost all opportunistic infections is extremely difficult because the person's immune system is usually so depressed that the invaders have "unlimited opportunities." In fact, the opportunities are so great that more than one opportunistic infection often takes hold in a person with AIDS. As a result, a person who has had AIDS for some time may have developed many opportunistic infections. At this point, the person is often weak, thin, almost lifeless, and close to death.

Because of the numerous opportunistic infections that may develop, AIDS is actually not a disease but a **syndrome**. Hence its name—acquired immune deficiency *syndrome*, and not acquired immune deficiency *disease*. A syndrome is a group of signs or symptoms that, taken together, indicate a certain condition or disease. Considering all the opportunistic infections that may develop, no condition has earned the name *syndrome* more than AIDS.

## The Impact of AIDS

The CDC estimates that 1 million people in the United States are infected with HIV. This means that 1 in every 250 people in the nation are infected with the virus that causes AIDS and can transmit HIV to others. In New York City alone, 1 in every 30 adults is infected with HIV. But adults are not the only people who need to be concerned about HIV infection. The number of HIV-infected teenagers in the United States doubles every 14 months. Currently, nearly 25 percent of new HIV infections are estimated to occur in young people aged 13 to 20.

The United States has the highest reported rate of AIDS in the industrialized world. This number varies from state to state. Some states have rates that are higher than those of some countries. For example, the rate of AIDS reported for Florida is higher than that for France. Those states with the highest rate have large urban areas, while those with the lowest rates are mainly rural. Obviously, the more closely together people live, the greater the chances of transmitting a contagious disease. Every 13 minutes, someone in America is infected with HIV.

Through 1999, a total of nearly 730,000 cases of AIDS had been reported in the United States. This number was six times greater than that recorded for Brazil, the country with the second-highest number of AIDS cases in the world, with slightly more than 100,000 cases. The number for the United States was also nearly eight times greater than that recorded for Tanzania, the country in Africa with the highest number of reported AIDS cases, with a little over 82,000 cases. In the United States, AIDS is now the second leading cause of death for all Americans between the ages of 25 and 44. Every 15 minutes, someone in America dies of an AIDS-related disease (an opportunistic infection).

Of the 600,000 AIDS cases reported to date in the United States, 84 percent were males over the age of 13, 15 percent were females over the age of 13, and 1 percent were children under age 13. To date, nearly 340,000 of these people have died of an AIDS-related disease. In 1995, approximately 50,000 Americans with AIDS died. In 1996, this number dropped to 38,780. In 1997, slightly more than 14,000 people died of AIDS. In 1999, the National Center for Health Statistics reported that since 1995 deaths due to AIDS dropped more than 70 percent in the United States. Does this mean that scientists and doctors are "winning the war" against AIDS? Most would say that some of the "battles" that have been fought in this war are finally being won. As you will shortly see, the treatment to stop the spread of HIV in the body has improved. So, HIV-infected people are living longer.

Worldwide, the CDC estimates that slightly more than 9 million people have died from AIDS and some 30 million people are infected with HIV. This means that approximately 1 in every 100 adults aged 15 to 49 is infected with the virus. Half of these infections are believed to occur between the ages of 15 and 19. During 1997, almost 6 million people were found to have become infected with HIV—about 16,000 new infections every day. More than 90 percent of these new infections occurred in developing countries.

Unlike the first cases of AIDS discovered in the United States, more than 75 percent of all adult HIV infections resulted from heterosexual activities. Infection does not occur through casual, non-sexual contact with an infected person either at home or at school. More than 90 percent of HIV infections in infants and children are the result of mother-to-child transmission, which occurs either through birth or breast-feeding. As you will shortly see, treatment for infants and children with AIDS has not improved as much as treatment for adults with AIDS.

# Treatment

Treatment of AIDS is designed to inhibit the activity of HIV. If HIV can be kept in check, then the virus cannot destroy T-cells and other cells involved in the immune response. Thus, an HIV-infected person will be less likely to develop one or more opportunistic infections that may prove fatal. Scientists recognized that several approaches for an effective treatment could be tested. One approach could attempt to stop HIV from attaching to a host cell. A second approach could prevent the reverse transcriptase enzyme from working once the virus had successfully penetrated a host cell. Without this enzyme, HIV could not make the DNA that would eventually become part of the host cell DNA. This second approach has proved to be more successful.

A number of drugs have been designed to inhibit the activity of reverse transcriptase. One of the first virus inhibitors to be tested was a drug called zidovudine, more commonly known under its trade name AZT. A study done in 1987 showed that people with AIDS who took AZT lived longer and developed fewer opportunistic infections than those who did not take the drug. The results of a recent study suggest that taking AZT during pregnancy may help reduce the chance of transmission from an HIV-infected mother to her baby. Scientists have also discovered that AZT appears to work best when used in combination with another drug. This finding has lead to a search for a "drug cocktail" that would be the most effective in treating AIDS. Currently, five different drugs that inhibit reverse transcriptase are available to use in combination. The specific combination depends on a number of factors, including how far AIDS has progressed and how well the patient can tolerate the drugs.

Recently, a new group of drugs to treat AIDS has been developed. This group targets a different part of the life cycle of HIV. These drugs inhibit HIV from making and assembling the proteins it uses to make the viral coat. As a result, HIV cannot manufacture complete new viruses that can break open the host cell and infect other cells. Many people who have started taking these drugs experience fatigue and develop a skin rash during the first month. But these are people whose bodies have become resistant to reverse transcriptase inhibitors. The side effects are a small price to pay if these new drugs prove effective. Two recent studies show that a combination of two reverse transcriptase inhibitors and two protein inhibitors was most effective in keeping HIV in check. In patients treated with this combination, HIV was still present in their bodies but occupied very few cells.

Unfortunately, advances in treatment for infants and children have not equaled those for adults. Although AZT was approved in 1987 for use in adults, the drug was not available to children with AIDS until 1990 when additional tests had been completed. Because little is known about how the protein inhibitors affect children, their use in infants under two years old has not been approved. Even when the drugs are available, information is lacking about how best to use them. The effect of the drugs on the course of AIDS has been studied mainly in adults. This has left doctors guessing as to what combination and how much of each drug should be given to children with AIDS. The good news is that fewer than 500 HIV-infected babies were born in the United States during 1997. Four years earlier, nearly 2,000 HIV-infected babies had been born.

# The Future

Late in 1997, French scientists discovered something most unusual. Working in a hospital in Paris, they came across a man who remained totally free of HIV infection. This in itself was nothing unusual. However, what struck them was the fact that the man should definitely have been infected with HIV. He admitted to having frequent sexual contact, without any form of protection, with several homosexual partners who were all HIV infected. Laboratory tests revealed that the man possessed two unusual genes. These genes are responsible for making the protein on the surface of T-cells that HIV recognizes. This man's genes were different, causing the protein to have a different shape. Apparently, HIV could not recognize and bind to this man's T-cells.

Other interesting cases have been discovered in which a person has been infected with HIV but has yet to develop AIDS. Probably the longest documented case of an infected person who shows no signs of AIDS is a homosexual man who tested positive for HIV nearly 20 years ago. The man's CD4 count is 1,000, indicating that his immune system is normal. Scientists are actively studying such people where HIV has failed to damage or destroy their immune system. Another such person is a 43-year-old woman who became HIV infected from a blood transfusion. The woman shows no signs of AIDS. However, the blood donor died from AIDS as did two other people who received transfusions from the same donor. None of her four children, who were all breast-fed, nor her husband are infected with HIV. Perhaps people such as these will provide scientists with clues as to how to cure AIDS.

# 8 RELATIVE UNKOWNS

The STDs that you have read about in the previous chapters are diseases that many people have heard about. Some STDs, however, are relatively unknown. Although they may not have the notoriety that gonorrhea, syphilis, herpes, hepatitis, and AIDS have, these relative unknowns are not uncommon. In fact, one of these relative unknowns is believed to be the most widespread of all STDs. This STD is known as **chlamydia**.

## Chlamydia

Chlamydia is an STD caused by a bacterium called *Chlamydia trachomatis*. Until about 20 years ago, even doctors did not know much about this STD, perhaps because chlamydia is one of the hardest STDs to detect. Most people who are infected with the bacteria do not develop any symptoms of the disease and obviously do not seek medical attention. Because most people who have the disease are unaware that they are infected, chlamydia has been called the "silent epidemic." The word *epidemic* reflects the fact that chlamydia has become an extremely common STD. The CDC estimates that more than 4 million new cases of chlamydia occur each year in the United States. Any sexually active person can get the disease. Nearly half of sexually active teenagers are believed to be exposed to chlamydia. Unless chlamydia is treated, the disease may have a lifelong impact on a person, especially on women who plan to have children.

*Chlamydia is the most commonly diagnosed STD among sexually active young people.*

The chlamydia bacteria can live in semen, vaginal fluid, and blood. A person is at risk of acquiring chlamydia if he or she comes in direct contact with any of these body fluids from an infected person, usually through vaginal, oral, or anal sex. Like other STDs, chlamydia can also be transmitted from a pregnant woman to her newborn baby during delivery. Once inside the body, the bacteria can remain dormant for a long period of time before symptoms appear. Thus, most people who become infected with chlamydia do not feel anything at first. If symptoms do occur, they develop within one to three weeks after infection.

In men who develop symptoms, the chlamydia bacteria might cause the testes to swell. If left untreated for several years, the swollen testes can result in the male becoming sterile—he cannot have children. A male will also experience a discharge from his penis and pain when he urinates. Infected women often have no symptoms. If symptoms do occur, they may include a yellow discharge from the vagina, pain during urination, spotting of blood between menstrual cycles, nausea, and fever. The chlamydia bacteria can also cause an inflammation of the cervix and fallopian tubes. An infected woman also has a greater chance of having an ectopic pregnancy—a pregnancy where the baby develops in the fallopian tube rather than the uterus, as you read in Chapter 2. Ectopic pregnancies end in miscarriages and can be life threatening to the woman.

Even if the pregnancy is normal, the woman may transmit the disease to her newborn baby during delivery. Chlamydia bacteria can cause the child to develop a severe case of pneumonia and perhaps become blind. Because of these risks, many doctors recommend routine testing of all pregnant women for chlamydia. Untreated chlamydia in women can lead to pelvic inflammatory disease (PID). As you read in Chapter 2, PID may lead to infertility in a female by causing scarring of the fallopian tubes. Nearly 50 percent of all cases of PID are a result of a chlamydia infection.

Diagnosing a chlamydia infection is not easy because the symptoms, if they do appear, are similar to those caused by the gonorrhea bacteria. In fact, the two STDs often occur together. Doctors estimate 25 percent of men with gonorrhea and maybe as many as 50 percent of women with gonorrhea are also infected with chlamydia. To find out if a person has chlamydia, several different diagnostic tests are available. In one test, a sample of fluid is taken from a person's genital area and sent to a laboratory to be cultured. If the bacteria are present in the sample, technicians will be able to recognize them growing in the culture. Because it is difficult to grow chlamydia under laboratory conditions, the test results of a culture are not available for at least three days.

A test that was recently developed uses more sophisticated techniques, including dyes that can detect proteins present on the surface of the chlamydia bacteria. Although this test is slightly less accurate than the culture method, the results are available sooner. In addition the dye test can be

*Talk with your doctor if you have any reason to believe you have been exposed to an STD, even if no symptoms have appeared.*

performed as part of a routine medical examination and need not be sent out to a laboratory. The newest test for chlamydia involves checking for the bacteria in a person's urine. Although this test is much more costly, the results are available within four hours.

If the diagnosis is positive, then immediate treatment is advisable. In the past, a 7- to 10-day treatment with antibiotics was required. Tetracycline was the antibiotic of choice. However, if a person was allergic to tetracycline, then erythromycin was prescribed. New medications have reduced the amount of time that the person must take the antibiotic. For example, an antibiotic called azithromycin need be taken for only one day to treat a chlamydia infection. By the way, penicillin is not effective against chlamydia. Thus, if a person with gonorrhea is being treated with penicillin, a test for a chlamydia infection is most important. In that way, the person is sure to get the right antibiotic to treat the chlamydia infection.

Any antibiotic that is given to treat chlamydia— or any STD—should be taken as long as the doctor prescribes it, even after all symptoms disappear. Because they are contagious, people being treated for chlamydia should not engage in any sexual activity. This will help to reduce the spread of chlamydia, but unfortunately it will not *stop* the spread of this STD. Recall that most people with chlamydia do not develop symptoms. Yet these people are contagious and continue to transmit chlamydia bacteria to others. In an attempt to stop the spread of the "silent epidemic," doctors recommend that any person who has more than one sex partner be tested regularly for chlamydia.

# Chancroid

Another relatively unknown STD is **chancroid**. Chancroid is caused by a bacterium called *Hemophilus ducreyi*. This STD is not known to be transmitted in any way other than through vaginal, oral, or anal sex. Chancroid is found primarily in tropical areas of Africa, Asia, and South America, but several small outbreaks have occurred in the United States, Canada, and some European countries. In these countries, most people infected with chancroid contracted the disease on their travels to tropical countries. Once very common, chancroid is now reported to affect fewer than 1,500 Americans each year.

The incubation period for the chancroid bacteria is 3 to 14 days. The first symptom is a small bump on the penis, scrotum, or vagina. Within one day, the bump grows dramatically to form an **ulcer**. When you hear the word "ulcer," you probably think stomach problems. Actually, an ulcer is an inflammation that can occur in an area that lines the inside of the body or on the surface of the skin. The cells that are affected die, leaving a visible sore or scar. An ulcer caused by a chancroid infection is painful and bleeds easily if it is rubbed. About half the men infected develop one ulcer. Infected women frequently have four or more ulcers that may also appear on the inner thighs. Fortunately, women are less likely to develop ulcers. But women with chancroid may have pain when they urinate, rectal bleeding, or a discharge from the vagina.

The bacteria can spread in a person though secondary contact—touching an ulcer and then touching another part of the body. If the bacteria are spread to the mouth, an ulcer may form there. No matter where they form, chancroid ulcers put a person at a higher risk for becoming infected by HIV. The breaks in the skin provide a better opportunity for HIV to penetrate the body.

At first, the chancroid ulcer that appears resembles a chancre, the typical sore that develops in people with syphilis. However, the ulcer that forms in the later stages of chancroid is so characteristic that some doctors can diagnose the disease just from its appearance. To confirm the diagnosis, a doctor can take a sample from an ulcer and send it to a laboratory for analysis. If chancroid bacteria are present, they will appear in the culture within three days. A test that uses antibodies to detect the bacteria is also available. If the test result is positive, treatment should begin immediately.

If left untreated, chancroid may spontaneously heal itself without causing any complications. This healing process occurs in about half of those infected. Without proper medical treatment, however, chancroid ulcers may become infected with pus and leave deep scars in the infected areas. Therefore, medical treatment is highly recommended for all people infected with chancroid. This STD is easily cured by various antibiotics, usually taken in some combination. Once treatment is started, the bacteria are quickly destroyed. If treatment begins early enough, scarring will be prevented or at least kept to a minimum.

## Genital Warts

You have probably seen a **wart**, either on your own body or someone else's. A wart is a noncancerous growth that usually appears on the hands or feet. Warts can form on other parts of the body, however. A wart that appears in a region of a sexual organ is known as a **genital wart**. Genital warts are caused by a virus called *human papillomavirus* (HPV). More than 50 different types of this virus have been identified and 14 of them can cause genital warts. A few types of HPV have been linked to cervical cancer.

HPV is spread through sexual contact. After invading the body, the virus infects only the topmost layer of skin on the penis, vagina, or cervix. Here the viruses enter their lytic cycle, producing more viruses and may cause the skin to grow and form a wart. Warts may form on other parts of the body through secondary contact. A pregnant woman who is infected may also pass the virus to her baby during delivery.

The simplest way to diagnose this STD is simply by looking at the warts, which have a distinctive appearance. Genital warts have a pinkish color and a cauliflower-like shape. They may not appear until two or three months after a person has been infected by the virus. Nonetheless, the person is contagious and can spread the virus to others through vaginal, oral, or anal sex. The warts may disappear by themselves in 6 to 12 months, or a doctor may want to remove them surgically. Another option is to apply an antiviral drug to the wart. But once the HPV virus has invaded the body, it cannot be eliminated. Thus, the warts will come and go, just as the sores caused by the herpes virus do.

## Trichomoniasis

You read in Chapter 1 that STDs may be caused by bacteria, viruses, protists, and yeasts. But so far all the STDs we have discussed have been caused by either a bacterium or a virus. **Trichomoniasis**, simply referred to as "trick," is an STD that is caused by a protist called *Trichomonas vaginalis*. The name of the protist tells you how the disease got its name.

By looking at its name, you can also tell what part of the body is affected by trichomoniasis—the vagina. Trichomoniasis is an STD that mainly affects women. But men can also get the disease. The microorganism can be transmitted from a woman's vagina to a male's urethra during sex. The protist can also survive for hours in a moist environment outside the body. So, almost any moist object, such as a washcloth or towel, that touches an infected area can transmit the disease. A pregnant woman who is infected can also transmit the protist to her newborn baby during delivery.

Like most STDs, trichomoniasis may be present without causing any symptoms. In fact, the protist may live in the vagina for years without giving any sign of its presence. If symptoms do occur in an infected female, they usually include a painful inflammation of the vagina, a yellowish, odorous discharge from the vagina, and discomfort during sex. Men who are infected rarely have symptoms. If they do, they may feel discomfort in the urethra and some pain in the tip of the penis, which can become inflamed.

Diagnosing trichomoniasis is simple. The protist is rather large and easy to identify in a culture of a sample taken from the vaginal discharge or the male's urethra. One drawback is that it may take up to two weeks to get the test results. Some doctors may examine the sample under a microscope in their office while they wait for the test result. If they spot the protist, they can begin treatment with a single dose of metronidazole, an antibiotic. This antibiotic often causes severe nausea. Because of the high dosage that is required, doctors may prefer to give it in smaller amounts over several days.

Although trichomoniasis is not serious and can be easily treated, the disease poses one problem. You read in Chapter 4 that a Pap smear is a test for cervical cancer that involves taking a sample from a woman's cervix. The presence of the trichomoniasis protist can interfere with this test by masking the presence of abnormal cells, thus giving a false negative result. In other words, precancerous conditions may exist, but the signs are hidden. On the other hand, the protist can also make normal cells look unusual. In this case, the Pap smear will give a false positive result. In other words, no cervical cancer is present, but the presence of abnormal cells may indicate that it is. For a woman infected with trichomoniasis then, any Pap smear should be postponed until the infection has been treated and cured.

## Yeast Infections

A **yeast infection** is an STD that occurs mainly in women. *Candida* yeast is normally present in small amounts in the mouth, digestive tract, and vagina where it usually causes no problem. However, under certain conditions, the yeast starts to divide rapidly, primarily in the vagina. As a result, its numbers increase dramatically and cause a yeast infection. Symptoms of a yeast infection include itching, burning, redness, and a cottage cheese-like discharge from the vagina.

Approximately 75 percent of all women experience at least one yeast infection during their lifetime. Although the yeast may be present in their bodies, men rarely develop an infection. If they do, the infection can develop in various parts of their bodies. You read in Chapter 7 how AIDS was first detected among a group of homosexual men with a yeast infection that had developed in their throats.

Certain conditions increase the chances of women developing a yeast infection, including the type of clothing they wear. Anything that can hold in heat and moisture, such as tight jeans and wet bathing suits, provides an ideal environment for the yeast. Because the yeast also thrive on sugar, cutting down on sweets can reduce the chances of developing a yeast infection. Yeast infections occur more frequently in women with **diabetes**. Diabetes is a condition in which the body cannot regulate the quantity of sugar that travels in the blood. At times, a diabetic may have a high blood-sugar level. This excess sugar can promote a yeast infection. Sugar levels also fluctuate during the menstrual cycle and pregnancy. Because the sugar level peaks at the midpoint of the menstrual cycle, a woman is more likely to develop a yeast infection at that time. Sugar levels are also highest during the last three months of pregnancy, so a yeast infection is more likely then. Finally, anyone taking an antibiotic is also more likely to develop a yeast infection. By killing bacteria that would otherwise compete with the yeast, the antibiotic "opens the door" for the yeast to multiply and spread.

Because of the way it develops, some people do not classify a yeast infection as an STD. True, a yeast infection can be transmitted through sexual contact. For example, a woman with a yeast infection may transmit the yeast to her sex partner who subsequently develops an itching, redness, and discomfort in his penis. Transmission through sexual contact, however, is rarely the cause of a yeast infection. Rather the infection results mainly from any change in environmental conditions that favor a rapid growth of the yeast.

Various creams are available to treat a yeast infection. Some of these are sold as over-the-counter medications. Care should be exercised when selecting such a medication. Some are intended merely to relieve the symptoms, while others are designed to cure the infection. Some creams used to treat a yeast infection are available only by prescription. Women who have repeated yeast infections may need an oral medication that is taken over an extended period of time. A woman should be aware that an over-the-counter medication used to treat a yeast infection of the vagina will be useless if the condition is caused by a bacterium.

Yeast infections conclude our look at STDs. You know the cause, transmission, diagnosis, symptoms, and treatments for a variety of STDs. But what we have not examined is perhaps the most important part of the story—how STDs can be prevented. After all, if an STD is prevented, a person need not worry about what the disease might do. The steps that prevent an STD are simple, as you will discover in the next chapter.

*In some cases a prescription for a yeast infection may be the best course of action.*

# 9 PREVENTING STDs

Between 10 million and 12 million Americans become infected with an STD every year. The only infectious diseases that affect more people are the common cold and the flu. Moreover, between 20 percent and 40 percent of American adults are estimated to be infected with an incurable STD, such as genital herpes, hepatitis B, genital warts, and HIV. According to a 1998 research study, the annual cost of treating all STDs contracted by Americans is more than $8 billion. These numbers are amazing considering how simple it would be to stop the spread of STDs. All a person need do is avoid contracting and, in turn, spreading an STD. It can be summarized in just one statement: *Be defensive.* You may have heard the terms "go on the defensive" or "defensive driving." Both these terms refer to situations where people take whatever action is necessary to avoid a danger, a problem, or a catastrophe. For example, a military unit may "go on the defensive" to prevent defeat by the enemy. Someone who is behind the wheel of a car will practice "defensive driving" to prevent an accident that would really be someone else's fault. In other words, being defensive simply means that a person wishes to prevent something undesirable from happening. In the case of STDs, being defensive means taking whatever actions are necessary to prevent STD infections from spreading.

Being defensive does *not* mean that a person has to become physically and socially isolated from others. No one wants to be a recluse without friends or social contacts. Being defensive simply means using common sense to protect oneself from obvious dangers. Most of these dangers, especially when it comes to STDs, are easy to avoid. Being defensive also involves developing a sense of self-respect so that one feels worthwhile and important. This will mean that at times a person will have to disregard what others may say. Being defensive also involves developing an awareness that anyone can contract an STD. It can happen to you! Keep in mind that two-thirds of all new cases of STD infections occur in people under age 25. One-fourth of all new STDs occur in teenagers. By the time they are 21, one in five teenagers has been treated for an STD.

In spite of these numbers, teenagers still feel invincible. They hear about others contracting an STD or read about some teenager being injured in a car accident. But they do not believe that anything so terrible can happen to them. But just think back to the story of Greg H. in Chapter 4. Greg never thought he would have an STD for the rest of his life simply by having sex that night on the beach. Being defensive means exercising some control over the way you live. This involves saying "no" when everyone else seems to be saying "yes." This also means not giving into peer pressure, which is the most difficult thing for a teenager to do.

Being defensive against STDs involves just three steps. In fact, if you follow the first step, there is no need to pay any attention to the other two steps. As you have read in the previous chapters, pathogens that cause STDs can invade the body in several ways. So, all you have to do is take the first step, which will effectively block all the "avenues" that are used by a pathogen to enter the body.

## Step 1: Just Say "No"

Undoubtedly you have heard the expression "Just say no." In the case of STDs, this applies to both drugs and sex. By simply saying "no" to drugs and premarital sex, you will prevent pathogens from penetrating the barrier that your body has erected. You have read that some STDs, especially HIV and hepatitis B, can be transmitted by contaminated needles that are used to inject drugs. If a needle is used by someone infected with an STD, the traces of blood that stick to the needle may contain the pathogen. If someone else uses the same needle, that person may wind up injecting the pathogen directly into his or her body. People who are addicted to drugs are especially vulnerable to STDs that are acquired through "dirty" needles. Thousands of addicts have become infected with HIV and hepatitis simply because they used "dirty" needles to inject drugs into their bodies. In an attempt to reduce the spread of STDs, drug-rehabilitation programs have provided addicts with clean needles while they go through withdrawal. Obviously the wisest step is never to start using drugs, especially drugs that are injected.

Those who work in the health-care field, including doctors and nurses, must use caution whenever their work involves the use of a needle. If you have recently received an immunization or any type of injection, you probably noticed how careful the doctor or nurse was when handling the needle. They used latex gloves to prevent any blood from entering their bodies, and they carefully disposed of the used needle. Unfortunately, even with all these precautions, some health-care workers have become infected with HIV or hepatitis B. Either they accidentally poked themselves with a needle or someone else accidentally stuck them. In some cases, the needle had traces of infected blood. As a result, these workers became infected with hepatitis B or HIV. Some of those infected with HIV have developed AIDS.

It is important, however, to avoid using any unprescribed drug, not just those that are injected. Consider what might happen when someone uses a "recreational drug" such as marijuana, cocaine, or even alcohol. Any of these drugs, especially if taken in large doses, affect the brain and thus one's judgment of right and wrong. As a result, the person is not able to use reason and common sense. Recall that Greg H. and his friends were drinking that night on the beach. No doubt this affected their judgment. If he had not been drinking, Greg may have thought twice about having sex with a girl he had just met. This applies to females, too. In fact, sexual contact results in females becoming infected with an STD more often than males.

When drugs are not involved, saying "no" can still be very difficult. This is especially true of teenagers because they have just entered the stage of their life when sexuality is developing. As they enter their teens, young people begin to sense an unusual feeling—the development of an interest in sex. Interest in sex is a result of chemical and physical changes taking place in their bodies. As they enter their teen years, **hormone** levels begin to rise. A hormone is a chemical substance produced in the body that brings about a specific result. For example, teenaged boys develop increasingly higher levels of a male hormone called **testosterone**. Testosterone

*Many teenagers today are likely to experience sex–and possibly, an STD–soon after puberty.*

causes their voices to deepen and enables their testes to produce sperm. Teenaged girls develop increasingly higher levels of a female hormone called **estrogen**. Estrogen causes their breasts to enlarge and their bodies to prepare for a possible pregnancy. With all these changes taking place, it is no wonder that sexual urges are very powerful.

But the possibility of contracting an STD is a very good reason to hold these feelings in check and postpone sex until reaching a more mature age. Obviously, teenagers who decide to postpone sex, at least for the time being, do not have to worry about contracting an STD. The possibility of contracting an STD, however, is not the only reason for postponing sex. A sexual relationship almost always

124

involves very strong emotions and the breakup of such a relationship can be very upsetting and have a long-lasting effect. Someone is likely to be angry and hurt, and these feelings may affect some future relationship.

Starting a sexual relationship as a teenager can also result in an unwanted responsibility—an unplanned pregnancy. Having to deal with the changes and responsibilities of growing up is hard enough without having to worry about the responsibility for a baby before one is ready and able to do so. Saying "no" to sex as a teenager may not only prevent getting an STD but may also avoid a number of other problems. But if saying "no" to sex seems impractical or impossible, a person has to proceed to the second step to prevent contracting an STD.

## Step 2: Practice Safe Sex

Safe sex means just doing what is necessary to protect both oneself and one's sex partner from getting an STD. The first thing is to develop and keep a **monogamous** sexual relationship. This simply means that each person has only one sex partner and is not **promiscuous** by having sex with several different partners. Common sense points out that the more sex partners a person has, the greater the risk of becoming infected by an STD. A much smaller risk comes when a person has only one sex partner who is also monogamous. In addition, the more a person knows about his or her sex partner, the smaller the risk of contracting an STD. For example, being aware that someone has had a number of sexual relationships with others in the past may make someone think twice before having sex with that person. For this reason, two people should openly discuss any sexual relationships they may have had in the past.

However, what a person says about their sexual relationships may not be the truth. People tend to lie about their sexual practices. In a recent survey of sexually active students, researchers asked both males and females how they went about deciding whether to have sex with somebody. Most of the students said that they openly discussed their past sexual histories with a prospective sex partner. However, the same study revealed that 75 percent of the male students interviewed, and about 50 percent of the female students, had lied to their prospective sex partners. They said they had lied because they felt that telling the truth would ruin their chances of having sex. The best solution to this problem is to establish a fairly lengthy and non-sexual friendship with a person before actually having sex. In this way, a person will have a better and more accurate guide to the sexual history of their prospective sex partner. What this means is rather than simply saying "no" to sex, all a person has to do is say "no, at least for the time being." If a prospective sex partner admits to having an STD, then sex is out of the question until medical treatment is completed and the person is cured. Of course, if the STD cannot be cured, then the two people will have to think about the possible consequences of having sex, especially if they do not practice safe sex.

Whenever the relationship has developed to the point where two people decide to have sex, then safe sex means taking certain protective measures. The risk of contracting an STD can be greatly limited by using a **condom**, which is commonly referred to as a "rubber." A condom is a tube of very thin latex rubber, closed at one end, which is rolled down over an erect penis before having sex. The condom prevents direct contact between the penis and vagina. Studies have shown that the pathogens that cause STDs, even the tiny viruses that cause hepatitis and AIDS, cannot penetrate latex rubber. Thus, even if a person is infected, there is little risk that he or she will transmit the pathogen to their sex partner. But this applies only to latex condoms. Some condoms, which are known as "natural" condoms, are made from lamb skin and contain tiny pores. These condoms are useless in preventing an STD infection because those tiny pores allow pathogens to pass through the lamb skin.

Used consistently and correctly, latex condoms have been shown to provide up to 99 percent protection against most STDs, including HIV. In the

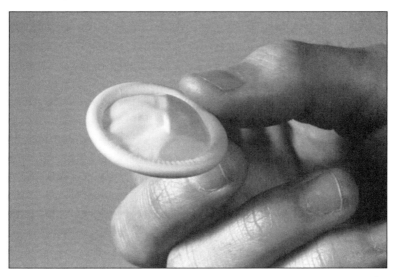

*Latex condoms are the only birth control devices that also help prevent an STD.*

case of a male, the condom must be placed on the penis before any sexual contact is made. The condom should be rolled all the way down the penis, leaving a small space at the tip to reduce the chance of causing a tiny tear in the latex during sex. Oils and oil-based products should not be used as a lubricant because they can weaken the condom. The condom must be kept in place as long as the penis is in the vagina. Following ejaculation of the semen, the penis should be withdrawn as soon as possible. In this way, the penis will not become soft inside the vagina where the condom may become loose and leak. A female can also insert a diaphragm over her cervix as a barrier against STD-causing pathogens that may be present in the semen.

The risk of infection is further reduced if a condom is used along with a **spermicide**. A spermicide is a jelly or foam that contains a chemical designed to kill sperm and thus reduce the chances of a woman becoming pregnant. A spermicide can either be coated on the condom or applied to the vagina. The chemical in a spermicide also kills many of the pathogens that may be present in the semen. Thus, a spermicide reduces the chances of becoming infected with an STD.

Despite their effectiveness, condoms are seen as a nuisance by many people. These people find it a hassle to keep a condom handy just in case they decide to have sex. Many people also feel that carrying a condom in their wallet or purse makes it look as if they are ready to have sex with anyone. Many men also do not want to stop and take the time to put on a condom when their sexual urges advise them otherwise. Some females feel that the spontaneity of sex is lost when their sex partners take the time to put on a condom properly. Both sexes may also feel that the use of a condom dulls the sensations that they would otherwise have. But the simple fact is that safe sex, including the use of a condom, is guaranteed to reduce the risk of contracting an STD. If a condom is not used, a person may have to face the next step, which is aimed at treating an STD and preventing its spread.

## Step 3: See a Doctor

Anyone who suspects that they have been infected with an STD should see a doctor or other health care provider as soon as possible. You have read that symptoms may not always appear after infection by an STD pathogen. Recall, for example, that most people infected with chlamydia do not develop any symptoms. Understandably, these people may

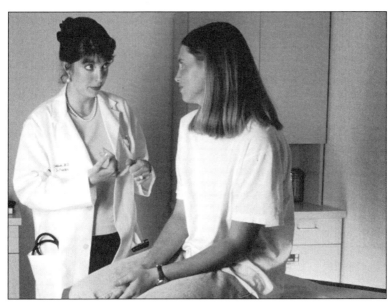

*A doctor you trust can help you to protect your sexual health—and perhaps even save your life.*

129

not seek medical attention unless they see their doctor for a routine medical examination that reveals an STD infection. But if any of the warning signs of an STD infection appear, a person has no excuse for failing to see a doctor as soon as they can. "Warning signs" of an STD infection include: abnormal discharges; painful or burning urination; sores, bumps, or blisters on genitals; itching in the genital area; abnormal monthly bleeding; painful intercourse; and unexplained skin rashes.

Bear in keep in mind that any information shared between a patient and a doctor or health-care provider is confidential. No one should find out the reason for the visit to a doctor's office, unless the patient decides to tell someone else. But if a person still feels uncomfortable or embarrassed about seeing a family or local doctor, he or she can go to a public health service STD clinic. Another reason for visiting a clinic may be the cost. All large cities and most smaller cities have clinics that do not charge anything. A doctor at the clinic will also keep any information confidential. All that the clinic may do is report the STD as a statistic—with no names—to the Centers for Disease Control. In this way, the CDC can keep track of STDs and determine whether any of them are reaching epidemic proportions.

No matter where a person goes to check on a possible STD infection, the same process will take place. First, the doctor or health-care provider asks the patient a number of questions, including questions about their recent sexual activities. Next, a medical examination is performed with special attention given to the genital areas for possible signs of infection. If any sores, blisters, or rashes are present, the doctor may take a sample and send it to a

130

laboratory for culturing. A blood sample is also taken and sent to the laboratory for analysis. If any of these tests reveal an STD infection, the doctor will prescribe the proper medication. The type of medication prescribed depends on whether the pathogen is a bacterium, virus, protist, or yeast. The patient must be sure to take the medication for as long as the doctor prescribed and not stop taking it because they start to feel better or because signs of the infection start to clear up.

To prevent the spread of an STD, medical personnel will also try to contact anyone who has had sex with the infected person so that they too can be treated. Obviously, the patient must be completely honest when answering questions that deal with their sexual activities. Only in that way can doctors treat the person responsible for infecting the patient and anyone whom the patient may have in turn infected. This is the only way to stop or control the spread of STDs.

# Glossary

*acquired immune deficiency syndrome (AIDS)*—STD caused by the human immunodeficiency virus (HIV), which attacks and destroys the immune system

*anemia*—lack of sufficient oxygen in the blood

*aneurysm*—swelling or ballooning of a blood vessel that may burst

*antibiotic*—chemical substance used to kill bacteria

*antibody*—protein produced by white blood cells in response to a pathogen or anything foreign that enters the body

*antigen*—anything that brings about an immune response

*antiviral drug*—drug designed to inhibit the reproduction of viruses in the body

*aorta*—major artery that exits the heart bringing blood to all body parts except the lungs

*bacterium (bacteria, plural)*—single-celled organism; the simplest form of life

*CD4 count*—number of CD4 T-lymphocytes per cubic millimeter of blood

*CD4 T-lymphocyte*—white blood cell that is a prime target for infection by HIV-1

*cardiovascular syphilis*—condition in which syphilis bacteria have invaded the heart or blood vessels during the last stage of the disease

132

*carrier*—person who carries the pathogen for a disease, perhaps throughout life, without showing any symptoms of the disease

*cervix*—lower end of the uterus

*chancre*—small, painless sore that often appears on the penis, vulva, or cervix during the first stage of syphilis

*chancroid*—STD caused by the bacterium *Hemophilus ducreyi*

*chlamydia*—the most common STD; caused by the bacterium *Chlamydia trachomatis*

*chronic hepatitis*—disease that affects a person who has carried the hepatitis B virus for at least six months

*cirrhosis*—condition in which liver cells are destroyed, preventing the organ from performing its various jobs

*condom*—device used as a birth-control method; also protects against an STD infection

*congenital syphilis*—presence of syphilis in a newborn baby as a result of an infected mother transmitting the disease to her child at some point during her pregnancy

*contagious disease*—disease that can be transmitted from one person to another

*cytomegalovirus (CMV)*—virus responsible for an opportunistic infection in people with AIDS

*deoxyribonucleic acid (DNA)*—one of the two types of nucleic acids

*diabetes*—disease in which the body cannot regulate its blood-sugar level

*disseminated gonorrhea*—gonorrhea that has spread throughout the body, affecting numerous organs and body parts

*ectopic pregnancy (tubal pregnancy)*—development of a fertilized egg in the fallopian tube or a site other than the uterus, often leading to a miscarriage

*enzyme*—chemical substance that speeds up the rate of a chemical reaction

*enzyme linked immunoabsorbent assay (ELISA)*—procedure to test blood for HIV infection

*epidemic*—contagious disease that spreads through human populations in a major geographic area

*estrogen*—female hormone whose level increases during adolescence

*fallopian tube*—narrow tube that connects the ovary on each side of the body to the uterus

*first episode*—first time a person experiences the symptoms of a herpes infection

*gene*—functional unit of heredity

*genital herpes*—incurable STD caused by a virus that produces sores and blisters on the sex organs

*genital wart*—noncancerous growth that appears on a genital area

*genitals*—sex organs

*gonorrhea*—one of the most common STDs; caused by a bacterium that mainly invades the urethra and the cervix

*hepatitis*—disease that affects the liver; caused by several different strains of a virus, including hepatitis B, which is sexually transmitted

*herpes simplex*—virus that consists of two strains

*herpes simplex virus type 1*—virus that generally infects the mouth region producing "cold sores"

134

*herpes simplex virus type 2*—virus that usually infects the sex organs producing blisters

*hormone*—chemical produced in one part of the body that brings about a specific result in another part of the body

*human immunodeficiency virus (HIV)*—virus that causes AIDS

*immune response*—attack launched by the body in response to invasion by a pathogen

*incubation period*—time that elapses between the initial infection and the first signs of a disease

*interferon*—protein the body produces in response to a viral infection

*jaundice*—yellowish tinge to the skin or eyes caused by hepatitis

*lymphocyte*—white blood cell that is part of the immune system

*lysogenic cycle*—phase in which a virus incorporates its DNA into the host cell's DNA without causing any immediate destruction to the cell

*lytic cycle*—destructive phase of viral infection in which a virus takes over the host cell's "machinery"

*macrophage*—white blood cell that is a prime target for infection by HIV-1

*meningitis*—inflammation of the membranes surrounding the brain or spinal cord

*microorganism*—tiny living thing that is often made up of a single cell; it can be seen only with a microscope

*mitosis*—process by which one cell divides to produce two cells

*monogamous*—having only one sexual partner

*neurosyphilis*—condition in which syphilis bacteria have invaded the nervous system, including the brain, during the last stage of the disease

*nucleic acid*—chemical substance involved in passing hereditary information from one generation to the next

*nucleotide*—chemical building block of both DNA and RNA

*opportunistic infection*—infection that develops because of a depressed immune system caused by HIV infection

*ovary*—female sex organ where eggs are produced

*pandemic*—worldwide epidemic

*Pap smear*—test for cervical cancer

*pathogen*—any organism or particle that causes a disease or infection in another organism

*pelvic inflammatory disease (PID)*—infection that affects a female's fallopian tube; usually the result of an STD

*penis*—male sex organ

*primary contact*—means by which a person becomes infected because of direct physical contact with another person

*primary infection*—first time a person becomes infected with the herpes virus, usually producing no symptoms

*promiscuous*—having several sexual partners

*protist*—organism that consists of a single cell but is more complex than a bacterium

*receptor*—surface protein on a cell that can bind to a pathogen

*recurrent episode*—reappearance of the symptoms of a herpes virus infection

*retina*—light-sensitive part of the eye

*retrovirus*—virus that contains RNA, and not DNA, as its genetic material

*reverse transcriptase*—enzyme that can make DNA from RNA

*ribonucleic acid (RNA)*—one of the two types of nucleic acid

*scrotum*—pouch of skin that holds a testis outside the body

*secondary contact*—means by which an infection can be spread to another part of the body

*semen*—fluid that contains sperm

*septic arthritis*—infection of the joints by gonorrhea bacteria, resulting in pain and limited mobility

*septicemia*—blood poisoning

*sexually transmitted disease (STD)*—disease that can be acquired as a result of vaginal, oral, or anal sex

*sperm*—male reproductive cell

*spermicide*—chemical designed to kill sperm; also kills many STD pathogens

*syndrome*—group of signs or symptoms that indicate a certain condition or disease

*syphilis*—one of the oldest known STDs caused by a bacterium responsible for a disease that progresses through several stages

*testis* (testes, plural)—male sex organ where sperm are produced

*testosterone*—male hormone whose level increases during adolescence

*toxin*—poison that is secreted by an organism such as bacteria

*trichomoniasis*—STD caused by a protist

*ulcer*—inflammation in which cells die, leaving a sore or scar

*urethra*—external opening for urine in both males and females; in males, the urethra also serves as the exit for sperm

*uterus*—part of the female reproductive system that is commonly called the womb

*vaccination*—procedure used to immunize a person against a disease

*vagina*—muscular tube that is part of the female reproductive system and serves as the site where sperm enter

*vesicle*—fluid-filled blister that forms as a result of a herpes type 2 virus infection

*viral replication*—production of new viruses inside an infected cell

*virulence*—degree to which a pathogen can cause disease or death

*virus*—causative agent of an infectious disease

*vulva*—external female reproductive organ that covers the opening to the vagina

*wart*—mass of cells that form a noncancerous growth

*western blot*—procedure to test blood for HIV infection

*yeast*—single-celled organism that grows in colonies

*yeast infection*—infection that mainly occurs in women when yeast in the vagina divide rapidly

# FURTHER READINGS

Alvin, Virginia and Robert Silverstein, *Hepatitis*. Springfield, NJ: Enslow Publishers, 1994.

Greenberg, Lorna, *AIDS: How It Works in the Body*. Danbury, CT: Franklin Watts, 1992.

Jordheimi, Anne A., *Sexually Transmitted Diseases & Today's Youth*. Kettering, OH: PPI Publishing, 1993.

Jussim, Daniel, *AIDS & HIV: Risky Business*. Springfield, NJ: Enslow Publishers, 1997.

Little, Marjorie, *Sexually Transmitted Diseases*. Broomall, PA: Chelsea House Publishers, 1991.

Nash, Carol Rush, *AIDS: Choices for Life*. Springfield, NJ: Enslow Publishers, 1997.

Schwartz, Linda, *AIDS: First Facts for Kids*. Santa Barbara, CA: Learning Works, 1997.

# RESOURCES

## NATIONAL ORGANIZATIONS AND WEB SITES
American Social Health Association
P.O. Box 13827
Research Triangle Park, NC 27709
*http://www.ashastd.org/*
This site provides links to information and updated news about STDs, as well as a hotline for herpes and AIDS.

Centers for Disease Control and Prevention
1600 Clifton Road, NE
Atlanta, GA 30333
1-888-CDC-FACT
1-800-227-8922 (National STD Hotline)
*http://www.cdc.gov/nchstp/od/nchstp.html/*
This site has general information about STDs, including trends and treatments. You can also find a "spotlight" containing updated articles and links to other sites dealing with STDs.

The Johns Hopkins University School of Medicine
720 Rutland Avenue
Baltimore, MD 21205
*http://www.med.jhu.edu/jhustd/stdpage2.htm/*
This site is maintained by a research group  whose focus is on STDs.

National Institutes of Health
Bethesda, MD 20892
*http://www.nih.gov*
This site features more than 1,000 fact sheets, articles, and other documents on STDs.

STD Clinic Locator
*http://www.unspeakable.com/locator/nph-locator.cgi/*
Locate an STD clinic in your area simply by entering a city and state. The clinic can provide you with information about a particular STD. You can also test your knowledge by taking the STD quiz.

World Health Organization
*http://www.who.int/*
Click on the search button, enter the keyword "STD," and you'll be given a long list of updated links that provide information on the impact of STDs worldwide.

# INDEX

Drugs, 68-69, 71, 122-23

Ehrlich, Paul, 48
Enzyme linked immuno-
absorbent assay (ELISA
or EIA), 97, 98

Fallopian tubes, 20, *20*,
21, 23, 27-28, 110
Fleming, Alexander, 14-15,
*14*

Genes, 82-84, 107
Genital herpes, 51-52, 53,
54, 56-58, 120
Genital warts, 114-15, 120
Gonorrhea, 22-34, 41,
108, 110-11
Gottlieb, Michael, 92-94,
*93*, 100, 101
Gram, Hans, 12
Gram-negative cells, 12-
13, 15, 29
Gram-positive cells, 12-13,
15, 29
Gram stain test, 29, 45

Hepatitis, 64-76, 78, 108,
120, 127
B, 63, 64, 66-67, 69-73,
75-76, 86, 95, 122, 123
Herpes, 51-63, *53, 56, 78,*
79, 100-1, 108, 115
Herpes simplex, 53-57, 58,
59, 60
Human immunodeficiency
virus (HIV), 77-89, *87,*
97, 99, 105, 106, 114,
120, 121, 123, 127

Immune system, the, 13-
14, 18, 31-32, 44, 46, 50,
54, 55, 58, 60, 62, 64,

65, 66, 72, 74, 77, 80-82,
84-86, 94, 99, 100, 102
Influenza, 91-92, *91*
Interferons, 72-73

Jenner, Edward, 74-75,
*74*

Kaposi sarcoma, 94, *94,*
100
Koch, Robert, 10, 11

Lister, Joseph, 10, 11
Liver, 14, 42, 44, 67-70,
72, 73, 78
Los Angeles, California,
92-93, 94, 100
Lymphocytes, 84-85, 86,
92-93, 100, 105, 107
Lysogenic cycle, the, 79,
81, 82, 99
Lytic cycle, the, 78-79, 86,
115

Macrophages, 81, 85, 86
Mantle, Mickey, 65-66, *65*

Needles, hypodermic, 21,
71, 87, 88, 122-23
Neisser, Albert, 22-23
Nerve cells, 13, 54, 58, 60
Neurosyphilis, 44-45, 49
New York City, 49, 93-94,
100, 102
Nucleic acid, 17, 78, 83
Nucleotides, 83-84

Oral sex, 21, 23, 41, 42,
54, 71, 87, 113, 115
Ovaries, 20-21, *20*

Pap smears, 62, *62*, 117
Pasteur, Louis, 10, 11

Pelvic inflammatory disease (PID), 27, 110
Penicillin, 15, 22, 30, 31, 48, *48*, 49, 112
Penis, 18-19, *19*, 23, 24, 26, 29, 42, 51, 52, 55, 110, 113, 116, 118, 127, 128
Pneumonia, 12, 15, 17, 92, 93, 94, 99, 100, 110
Pregnancy, 124, 125
and chlamydia, 109
ectopic, 27-28, 110
and genital warts, 115
and gonorrhea, 24, *25*, 26, 42
and hepatitis, 71, 75
and herpes, 60-61
and HIV, 88, 104, 105, 106, 107
and syphilis, 42
and trichomoniasis, 116
and yeast infections, 118
Privacy, 32-33, 130
Protein inhibitors, 106
Proteins, 17, 46, 72, 80, 81, 84, 86, 95, 106, 111
Protists, 16, 101-2, 115-17

Rashes, 42, 43, 44, 45, 46, 49, 106, 130
Receptors, 84-85
Retroviruses, 79, 82
Reverse transcriptase, 79, 80, 81, 84, 85-86, 105, 106
Ribonucleic acid (RNA), 17, 78, 79, 81-82, 85-86

"Safe sex," 34, 125-29
Semmelweis, Ignaz, 11

Septic arthritis, 26-27
Serum hepatitis, 66
Sterility, 110
Syphilis, 35-50, *40, 41, 45, 48*, 90, 108, 114

Trichomoniasis, 16, 115-17
"Tuskegee Study of Untreated Syphilis in the Male Negro," 37-40, *40*

Urethra, 19, *19*, 23, 26, 27, 30, 116
Urination, 19, 21, 26, 27, 58, 69, 70, 110, 112, 113, 130

Vaccinations, 18, 73-76, *74*, 86
Vagina, 20, *20*, 21, 27, 29, 30, 58, 60, 71, 87, 109, 113, 116, 117, 119, 127
Vaginal sex, 23, 41, 54, 69, 115
van Leeuwenhoek, Anton, 9-10
Vesicles (blisters), 51, 53, *53*, 56, *56*, 57, 58, 59, 61, 63, 115, 130
Viral replication, 78-79, 80
Viruses, 17-18, 53, 59, 61, 62, 64, 72, 77-89, 91, 100, 101, 115
Vulva, 20, *20*, 24, 42, 55

Western blot, 97-98

Yeast infections, 16-17, 92, 93, 101, 115, 117-19, *119*

# ABOUT THE AUTHOR

After teaching high school biology and chemistry for 25 years, Salvatore Tocci now devotes his working time to writing science books. Since his retirement, Mr. Tocci has served as senior author on a high school chemistry text and has written 8 books for middle school and high school students. He is currently writing a series of 14 science books for students in grades 3 to 5. A resident of East Hampton, New York, he spends his spare time during the winter months working in his darkroom and constructing his 12 X 24 HO train layout. During the warmer times of the year, he and his wife Patti spend time on their sailboat, the *Royal T*.